GLOBAL SERVICE
MANAGEMENT
PRINCIPLES AND PRACTICES

Hak-Seon Kim, Seieun Kim, Aura L. Riswanto
Angellie Williady, & Hyun-Jeong Ban

BAEKSAN

Prologue

This book is designed to help readers acquire theoretical knowledge of service management and apply it in practice, serving as a guideline for corporate management in the service industry. It begins with a definition of service management, followed by the second chapter on understanding service customers and the third chapter on customer relationship management. It then addresses issues related to service differentiation, studies related cases, and discusses service marketing, service quality, and service leadership. The final chapter covers an introduction to customer satisfaction management.

Drawing from our experience in lecturing and researching service management, we have referred to both domestic and international books, papers, and case studies to convey knowledge on service management and to enhance readers' perspectives and insights on the subject. However, we plan to continue developing this work through ongoing research and incorporating readers' feedback. We hope this book will be utilized by not only undergraduate and graduate students but also practitioners in the service industry to improve services and generate innovative ideas. Lastly, we would like to express our gratitude to everyone who contributed to the publication of this book.

August, 2024

The Authors

Contents

C·o·n·t·e·n·t·s

Understanding Service Management

Understanding Service Management

Chapter **1**

1.1 Fundamental Concepts of Service

(1) Origin of Word − "Service"

This word originates from the Latin word *Servus*, meaning "slave". Later, the word evolved into "to help someone", resulting in words like "servant" and "servitude". It originally meant "slave loyalty", however, now it has evolved to mean "help" and further to the meaning of "costless".

(2) Changes in the Perception of Service

① Medieval to Modern Times

Service was seen as a non-productive and not very important area.

② Industrial Society

Initially, service was viewed as a supporting function of product sales, but has since gained value and grown into its own industry.

③ Modern Society

As time has progressed, the concept of service has gradually evolved into the concept of "serving others". It is widely accepted that service plays a fundamental and crucial role in all industries as an intangible value. Services have gained economic importance in recent years, resulting in a "service society" in which daily life is reliant on services. As a result, modern businesspeople must appreciate the value of service, treat their customers with humility and care, and anticipate their needs before they occur.

1.2 ⟶ Definition of Service

(1) Overview

① Definition of Service

The meaning of service has evolved significantly, now representing the dedication and effort used for the benefit of others. Dr. Schweitzer, a renowned philanthropist stated "The best thing a human can do is to serve others".

The fundamental understanding and spirit of service begin with respect and consideration expressing gratitude through actions. This approach creates a cycle where the joy is given to others returns as personal satisfaction.

Ultimately service can be defined as "an intangible product provided through interactions between humans or with facilities to satisfy people's needs".

② Composition of the Word "SERVICE"

S	Sincerity	Service filled with sincerity, speed, and smiles
E	Energy	Service full of lively energy
R	Revolutionary	Service that always provides something new and innovative
V	Valuable	Service that adds value to the customer
I	Impressive	Memorable service
C	Communication	Service that facilitates communication
E	Entertainment	Thoughtful and considerate service

(2) Economic and Business Administration Definitions of Service

In response to the growing importance of services in the economy and business of a nation, there is an increased interest in the service industry, and extensive research is being conducted in this field. Since services differ from tangible goods in many ways, scholars and practitioners are unable to agree on their definitions.

With the advent of the market economy paradigm, where suppliers are positioned to lead the market, the competition between suppliers has become more intense. There has been an increase in emphasis placed on hardware aspects of products, such as their inherent functions and quality. With prices and quality becoming increasingly important factors in consumer purchasing decisions, services have gained even more importance. Several major countries have a high employment ratio in the service sector, emphasizing its importance.

As early as the 1960s, researchers began studying services in the marketing field of business administration, focusing on the characteristics and phenomena of services in the 1970s. Academic research on the theoretical framework and strategic issues of services has become increasingly popular since the 1980s and 1990s. As of the mid-2000s, various policies have been implemented globally to promote the service industry.

| Service sector employment ratio of major countries |
(Unit: %)

Major Countries	2016	2017	2018	2019	2020
South Korea	69.96	69.91	69.80	70.28	69.98
France	77.14	77.11	77.41	77.31	78.03
Germany	71.31	71.32	71.41	71.62	-
United Kingdom	80.54	80.72	80.94	80.93	81.88
Italy	69.99	70.21	70.14	70.24	69.95
Japan	71.34	71.49	71.76	72.13	72.38

Source: Industrial Statistics Analysis System (2021)

The flow of services can be understood by examining the economic and managerial definitions as follows:

① Economic Definition

In economics, services are categorized as "intangibles" and are distinguished from tangible items. The economist Adam Smith[1] described services as "unproductive labor", while Say[2] defined them as "immaterial products". Fish and Clarke presented the major issues of growth, productivity, and employment within the context of economic development in order to clarify the meaning of services. As a result, services can be viewed as unproductive labor and immaterial goods from an economic standpoint. However, this viewpoint does not capture the true value of services for modern society as a whole.

---

1) Smith, A. (1776). *Wealth of Nations.*

2) Say, J. B.(1803). *A Treatise on Political Economy; or The Production, Distribution, and Consumption of Wealth.*

② Business Administration Definition

Comparing products and services has become a topic of academic research in the field of management since the 1960s.

a. Activity-Based Definition

As defined by the American Marketing Association, services include all activities, services, and benefits that are offered for sale or provided in connection with the sale of goods, including entertainment, hotels, electricity, transportation, beauty services, and credit services.The term "services" was defined by Stanton as intangible activities that meet the needs of consumers and may be sold independently of products.

b. Attribute-Based Definition

An intangible good sold in the market or "property without ownership" is a service that is distinguishable by whether or not it can be touched. A service is defined as "intangible goods sold in the market", and sometimes referred to as "property without ownership".

c. Service-Oriented Definition

Levitt[3] emphasized the benefits that the service provider provides to the service recipient, suggesting that industrialization of services could promote the efficiency of production.

d. Human Interaction-Based Definition

According to the definition of services, they are defined as a series of intangible activities that result from the interaction between the customer and the service employee, solving problems for the customer.

---

3) Levitt, T. (1976, September). The Industrialization of Service. *Harvard Business Review.*

1.3 · Background of Service Economy Growth

(1) Case study of South Korea – Aging Society

As of 2024, the number of elderly people aged 65 and over in South Korea is estimated at 9,938,235, making up 19.2% of the country's total population. Statistics Korea predicted that by 2025, this will rise to 20.3%, entering a super-aged society, and by 2036, it will reach 30.9%. As a result of advances in medical technology and improved living standards, the average life expectancy has increased to 83 years and the death rate has declined. The medical and retirement insurance industries, as well as specialized care facilities, are experiencing rapid growth in the silver sector as a result. Furthermore, educational services such as cultural centers and lifelong learning institutes are expanding for the elderly and highly educated.

| Trends and the Service Industry in the Aging Era |

Trends	Service Industry	Examples
Time Consumption (Long Life Expectancy)	• Experience Industry	• Travel and leisure • Silver entertainment and digital content
Beautiful Death	• Funeral Industry	• Nursing hospitals and nursing homes • Caregivers and social workers • Funeral halls
Healthy Aging	• Healthcare Industry	• Senior hospitals and elderly healthcare • Anti-aging industry
Social Activities	• Senior Community Industry	• Retirement communities (silver towns) • Remarriage services • Elderly recreational activities for socializing

(2) Diversity of Consumer Needs

A growing number of consumers have complex or heterogeneous needs, which makes it increasingly difficult to understand their demands. There has been a shift in priorities from a focus on basic physiological survival to a focus on enjoying life. As an example, restaurant visitors are now seeking dining experiences rather than simply meals in order to enhance their dining experience.

(3) Rapid Technological Advancements

The advancement and expansion of the information age are expected to further extend and grow the service sector due to social, economic, and cultural changes. This trend is predicted to accelerate even more with the development of digital information technology. In particular, the progress of digital technologies in the Fourth Industrial Revolution necessitates more sophisticated and differentiated technologies to meet consumer needs. The intelligence revolution driven by Information and Communication Technology (ICT) will create a highly connected foundation. This will enhance the convenience, safety, and richness of life through innovations like Artificial Intelligence (AI), Big Data, Cloud Computing, the Internet of Things (IoT), Blockchain, autonomous vehicles, wearables, Virtual Reality (VR), Augmented Reality (AR), and robotics.

(4) Increasing the Role of Women in Society

The desire for self-realization and the prevention of career interruptions have led to an increase in women's participation in society. In 2023, the economic activity participation rate of women in South Korea was 55.6% and has been steadily increasing. Additionally, the fields in which women are advancing are expanding.

Women, who possess abilities and qualities in areas such as emotional and aesthetic sense, and communication, are actively entering sectors like mass media, interior design, fashion, education, and healthcare. This trend is expected to stimulate demand in these fields and expand into new service industries.

(5) Pursuing Sustainable Management

The concept of sustainable management refers to corporate activities that are comprehensive and balanced in their consideration of economic, social, and ecological factors. This concept, known as "Servicizing", involves selling services rather than goods, allowing both producers and customers to benefit while protecting the environment. Examples include rental services, consulting, children's clothing lifespan extension services, and Samsung Electronics' total care service, which integrates the concept of preventive maintenance into its customer service structure, enhancing the added value of the service business.

1.4　Characteristics of Services

(1) Classification of Services

① Classification by Service Target

Services can be classified based on the type of input and the nature of the service outcome. Depending on whether the target of the service is people or products, services are categorized by the type of input. Additionally, services can be classified according to whether the results are tangible or intangible.

② Classification by Type of Service Industry

Classifying services by the type of service industry can be challenging, but it can be based on the number of customers a specific unit processes per day and the response patterns. Services can be divided into three types based on the characteristics of demand: professional services, store services, and mass services. The definitions of these service classifications are detailed in the table below.

| Characteristics of Demand by Service Industry Type |

Service Classification	Demand Characteristics
Professional Services	The service delivery process is important and centered around people. There is a long customer contact time, high customer demand, and employees have a lot of discretion. Example: Consulting, advisory firms
Store Services	Services are provided through a mix of people, equipment, and processes, having characteristics between professional services and mass services. Example: Banks, hotels
Mass Services	Limited customer contact time, minimal custom orders, and handling a large number of customers. Example: Railway companies, airlines, airport services

③ Schmenner's Service Process Matrix

Schmenner's Service Process Matrix classifies services based on two major dimensions that influence the service process. The horizontal axis is labor intensity, defined by the ratio of labor costs to capital costs. The vertical axis is the degree of customer interaction and customization. The Service Process Matrix divides services into four categories: service factory, service shop, mass service, and professional service. Their characteristics are as follows.

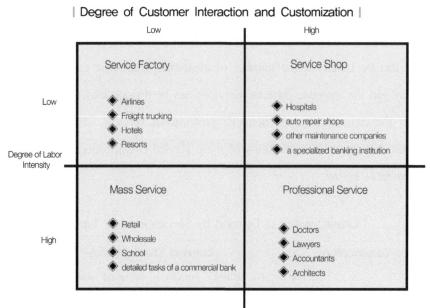

Source: Rorer W.Schmenner, "how can service Businesses survive and prosper?
Sloan Management Review, Vol.27, no. spring 1986, p.25

a. Service Factory: Characterized by low labor intensity and low interaction, providing standardized services in large quantities like a line-flow production factory. This category includes airlines, freight trucking, hotels, and resorts.

b. Service Shop: Characterized by low labor intensity and high interaction, offering highly customized services but requiring significant capital investment. Hospitals, auto repair shops, and other maintenance companies fall into this category.

c. Mass Service: Characterized by high labor intensity and low interaction, providing undifferentiated services in a labor-intensive environment. This category includes retail, wholesale, and education services.

d. Professional Service: Characterized by high labor intensity and high interaction, where professionally trained experts provide individualized services to customers. Doctors, lawyers, accountants, and architects belong to this category.

④ Classification by service delivery method

Classification by service delivery method depends on how the service is provided to customers, either at a single location or multiple locations. This relates to whether customers move to receive the service or the service company moves to provide the service to customers.

The disadvantage of a single location is that customer accessibility is lower compared to multiple locations. Multiple-location services involve providing services at various locations, making it more convenient for customers, but it poses a challenge for the service company in maintaining quality control across all sites.

| Classification by Service Delivery Method |

Interaction between Customers and Service Companies	Service Points	
	Single Location Services	Multiple Location Services
Customer Moves to the Service Company	Theater, barber shop, education	Bus, fast food, bank, hospital
Service Company Moves to the Customer	Taxi, event company	Mail delivery, local government office
Transactions via Information and Communication	Credit card, broadcasting station	Broadcasting network, telephone company

⑤ Classification by Service Function

Singleman's (J. Singleman) classification by service function is based on the argument that services are related to different economic activities and various social characteristics. Additionally, the classification by service function takes into account the relationship with national income based on employment.

| Classification by Service Function |

Classification by Service Function	Service Types
Distribution Services	Transportation, communication, trade services
Producer Services	Finance, corporate services, real estate
Social Services	Healthcare, education, postal, public and non-profit services
Personal Services	Hotel, food and beverage, travel, maintenance, and housekeeping services

⑥ Classification by the U.S. Census Bureau

The functional classification used by the U.S. Census Bureau for industry classification divides services into the following five categories. This functional classification is widely used in many countries around the world.

Classification of Services	Types of Services
Distribution Services	Services that assist in the movement of products or people, including transportation services and those provided by the information and data processing industry. Example) Airline services, communication services, delivery services.
Wholesale and Retail	Services that connect producers and consumers to provide convenience Example) Internet e-commerce, supermarkets, department stores
Non-profit Services	Services of nonprofit institutions or public interest organizations for the public interest Example)Volunteering, public service workers
Producer Services	Professional services to manufacturing or service industries Example) Finance, insurance, real estate, legal services
Consumer Services	Social and personal services provided to improve the quality of life Example) Medical care, education, car maintenance, other repairs

⑦ Lovelock's Classification[4]

In the foundational study on the classification of services within industrial societies, Lovelock criticized the existing classification systems for their lack of strategic insights into service marketing. Lovelock argued for a more comprehensive and sophisticated classification framework and consequently proposed the following five criteria for classification.

a. What are the nature of the service act?

Based on the object of the service act (whether it pertains to people or possessions) and the form of the service act (whether it is tangible or intangible), services can be categorized into the following four types.

Classification		Who or What is the Direct Recipient of the Service?	
		People	Possessions
What is the Nature of the Service Act?	Tangible Actions	Services directed at people's bodies • Medical services, beauty salons • Restaurants, barbershops • Passenger transportation, hotels	Services directed at goods and other physical possessions • Freight transportation • Laundry and dry cleaning • Industrial equipment repair and maintenance
	Intangible Actions	Services directed at people's minds • Education, Broadcasting • Theaters, Information services • Museums	Services directed at intangible assets • Banking, legal service • Accounting • Insurance

4) Lovelock, C. H. (1983). Classifying services to gain strategic marketing insights. *Journal of marketing, 47*(3), 9-20.

b. What type of relationship does the service organization have with its customers?

Classification		Type of Relationship between the Service Organization and Customers	
		"Membership" Relationship	No Formal Relationship
Nature of Service Delivery	Continuous Transactions	• Insurance, bank • Telephone subscription, college enrollment	• Broadcast, police protection • Public higway
	Discrete Transactions	• Long-distance phone calls • Transportation card	• Car rental • Mail service, toll highway • Movie theater, Restaurant

c. How Much Room for Customization and Judgment?

Services are produced and consumed simultaneously, and sometimes the customer directly participates in the production process. Therefore, there are various ways to tailor services to meet the needs of individual customers. To appropriately provide services according to customer orders, it is necessary to evaluate the nature of the service and the service delivery system. This evaluation includes assessing the level of service required by the customer and the degree of discretion the employees have to meet this level.

Classification		Extent to Which Service Characteristics Are Customized	
		High	Low
The Extent of Employee Discretion	High	• Legal services, Healthcare • Architectural design, Real estate agency	• Education (large classes) • Preventive health programs
	Low	• Hotels service • Fine dining restaurant	• Movie theater • Fast food restaurant • Public transportation

d. What Is the Nature of Demand and Supply for the Service?

Services that cannot keep an inventory of finished products are categorized based on how much demand fluctuates (a lot or a little) and supply limitations (whether they can immediately meet maximum capacity) as follows.

Classification		Extent of Demand Fluctuations over Time	
		Wide	Narrow
Extent of Supply	Peak Demand Can Usually Be Met	• Electricity • Telephone • Police and fire emergencies	• Insurance • Legal service • Laundry and dry cleaning
	Peak Demand Regularly Exceeds Capacity	• Accounting and tax preparation • Hotels • Theaters	Services similar to those above but which have insufficient capacity for their base level of business

e. How Is the Service Delivered?

Services are categorized into six types based on whether the service delivery points can be dispersed across multiple locations (single site or multiple set) and the nature of the contact between the service organization and the customer (customer visits the service provider, service provider visits the customer, or transactions occur at each party's location) as follows:

Classification	Single Site	Multiple Set
Customer Goes to Service Organization	• Theater • Barbershop	• Bus shop • Fast food chain
Service Organization Comes to Customer	• Lawn care service, Pest control service • Taxi	• Mail delivery • AAA emergency repairs
Customer and Service Organization Transact at Arm's Length	• Credit card company • Local TV station	• Broadcast network • Telephone company

(2) Service types classified by the type of control

① Company-Controlled Services

a. When a company emphasizes extreme efficiency, it may provide services centered around the company's needs.

b. The company must instill the perception that speed and economy are guaranteed.

c. Examples: Not providing shopping bags or not accepting credit cards at warehouse discount stores.

d. In this case, frontline employees have no autonomy and provide services mechanically according to the company's set manuals.

② Frontline Employee-Controlled Services

This type of service is controlled primarily by the frontline employees and is relatively rare. An example is face-to-face services provided by a one-person business. Too much autonomy may cause confusion for customers.

③ Customer-Controlled Services

Customer-controlled services are those where the main part of the service is controlled by the customer, and they can be divided into two dimensions:

a. Highly Standardized Service Process: When the service process is highly standardized and no frontline employees are needed, customers perform all the services themselves.

b. Reflecting Customer Intentions: In services like legal services, lawyers perform services reflecting the customer's intentions as much as possible.

(3) Characteristics of Services

① Basic Characteristics

  a. Intangibility: Services lack a physical form, making it necessary to present
     alternative physical evidence (such as colors, logos, etc.). They are difficult
     to protect through patents and have ambiguous pricing criteria. To address
     these issues, it's important to provide tangible evidence and images as
     practical cues, create concrete images through active communication, and
     pay attention to post-purchase communication.

  b. Perishability: Services cannot be stored or inventoried, and if not used
     immediately by the consumer, they perish. To overcome the perishability
     of services, it is essential to develop strategies that harmonize demand
     and supply.

  c. Inseparability (Simultaneity of Production and Consumption): Services
     are produced and consumed simultaneously in the same place, with the
     customer directly participating in the service provision. To address
     inseparability, it's important to utilize information technology or focus on
     the careful selection and thorough training of service providers.

  d. Heterogeneity: Services are highly dependent on the individuals providing
     them, making standardization difficult. The diverse needs, personalities,
     and customs of consumers lead to varied orders, and the individual traits,
     moods, friendliness, capabilities, and experiences of service providers
     result in differences in service. Therefore, it is necessary to build
     individualized strategies tailored to each customer segment from various
     perspectives.

| Characteristics of the Service, Issues, and Solutions |

Characteristics of Service	Issues	Solutions
Intangibility	• Cannot be stored • Cannot be displayed or transferred	• Provide tangible cues • Enhance personal contact and promote word-of-mouth • Create a strong corporate image
Perishability	• Cannot be stocked	• Balance between supply and demand • Develop strategies to handle demand fluctuations
Inseparability	• Consumer participation in production • Mass production is not possible	• Strengthen selection and training of front-line employees • Customer management
Heterogeneity	• Difficulty in standardization and uniformity	• Industrialization of services • Provide customized services

1.5   High-Quality Service

(1) Definition

While general service aims to perfectly meet the expressed needs of customers, high-quality service goes beyond this by adopting a customer-centric service philosophy that anticipates and satisfies even the unexpressed, latent needs of customers. This type of service not only achieves customer satisfaction but also delights the customer.

(2) One-Stop Service (Total Service)

① Concept

One-stop service refers to a setup where customers, upon visiting a company, hospital, etc., can handle all their needs in one place without having to go to multiple locations.

② Necessity

For customers, this service saves time and provides convenience by allowing them to handle everything at once. For companies, it offers significant benefits in terms of efficient resource allocation, improved operational efficiency, and enhanced customer satisfaction.

③ Methods

a. Provide customers with access to all desired services through a single, unified phone number.

b. When customers request services, set the necessary requirements consistently and provide the services, information, and materials from related organizations at a single location.

c. Assign a single point of contact or a dedicated department to each customer.

④ Success Factors

a. Leadership: Strong leadership is needed to clearly communicate the company's goals and vision, emphasizing the importance of one-stop service to employees and thoroughly educating them to motivate and align them with these objectives.

b. Data Management and Analysis: An efficient information system should be established so that employees can address any customer demands immediately. Continuous analysis and updates of data should be provided to keep the system effective.

c. Development and Management of Human Resources: After selecting competent personnel, a standard customer service manual should be created. Employees should be thoroughly trained and a culture of responsibility should be introduced. However, the goal of introducing this culture is not to hold employees accountable but to provide them with appropriate rewards and feedback for service improvement.

d. Process Management: Previously, companies operated efficiently through division of labor. Introducing one-stop service is a new innovation. Organizations are breaking down internal barriers and transforming through process management using information technology to provide perfect service.

e. Customer-Oriented Approach and Customer Satisfaction: It is necessary to constantly listen to customer needs, provide feedback, and reflect this in business operations to achieve customer satisfaction.

⑤ Characteristics

From the customer's perspective, a total service system can be broadly divided into three components: the service operations system, the service delivery system, and the service marketing system. A representative example of a total service is an airline.

(3) Examples

① Korean Airline's Total Service

"Customers are not satisfied with merely boarding and disembarking the plane". By providing personalized services to each customer through one-on-one service marketing, Korean Airline has achieved customer satisfaction. Major total services include: electric car services for pregnant women, the elderly, and people with disabilities; chat and text services for flight ticket reservations and purchases; international web check-in services, coatroom services, in-flight AVOD (Audio/Video On Demand) services and various events and promotional activities for customers.

② Asiana Airlines' Total Service

Asiana Airlines aims to "Scratch where the customers are itching" with its total service approach. Major services include: paid VIP transportation services with the luxury sedan, high-end sedan services instead of public transportation for arriving customers, celebrity security services, and specialized interpreter services for foreign passengers.

(4) Horizontal Human Relations Service

① Overview

To achieve customer satisfaction, one must be able to satisfy all of the customer's senses. In other words, one must be able to genuinely connect with the customer, which is possible only when engaging in a horizontal relationship rather than a vertical one. True service involves a horizontal relationship where opinions are exchanged equally, rather than a vertical relationship characterized by submissive obedience. Therefore, to provide proper service, it is essential to foster a spirit of mutual benefit rather than mere obedience.

② Methods to Captivate Customers

    a. Prepare Before Meeting the Customer: Anticipate and understand the customer's invisible feelings. Strive to do the best not only for current customers but also for potential future customers.

    b. Understanding the Customers with Your Heart, Not Just Your Head: Once you hurt the customer's feelings, your service will be seen as flawed, regardless of any technical excellence.

    c. Follow the Customer's Emotions: Customers inherently feel special. Align with their feelings and emotions.

    d. Customer is the Star of the Show: Do not outshine the customer, do not try to stand out more than the customer, and do not act superior to the customer. The customer should always be the one who shines the most.

(5) Example of High-Quality Service

① Waldorf Astoria Hotel

One stormy night in Philadelphia, an elderly couple arrived at a small hotel and asked the staff if there were any rooms available, even though they hadn't made a reservation. The staff member checked but found that there were no available rooms at his hotel or any nearby hotels. He told the couple, "We don't have any rooms, but it's stormy and very late—almost 1 a.m. I can't just send you out. It's not much, but you're welcome to stay in my room for the night". Although the couple initially declined, they eventually accepted the staff member's offer and spent the night in his room.

The next morning, as they were checking out, the elderly gentleman thanked the staff member, saying, "You should be the owner of the best hotel in America". Two years later, the staff member received a letter from the elderly gentleman, inviting him to visit New York and providing round-trip plane tickets. When the staff member arrived in New York, the elderly gentleman took him to a magnificent marble hotel and said, "I had this hotel built for you to manage". The hotel was the Waldorf Astoria. The elderly gentleman was William Waldorf Astor, the hotel's owner, and the staff member was George Bolt.

⑵ Stew Leonard Supermarket

Stew Leonard's Supermarket is an unusual store compared to typical supermarkets. It exclusively sells products like milk, orange juice, and coffee, and does not carry items such as seasonings, alcohol, or snacks. Although it offers only about 600 types of products-about 15% of what a typical supermarket offers-around 3.5 million customers visit each year, with some coming from as far as 30 kilometers away.

What made Stew Leonard's famous is the large 4-ton stone, known as the "Policy Stone", placed in front of the supermarket. This stone bears the following rules:

Rule 1: The customer is always right.
Rule 2: If something goes wrong, read 'Rule 1' again.

These rules are based on a painful experience of the founder, Stew Leonard. Early in the store's history, an elderly woman returned with eggs she had purchased the day before, claiming they were spoiled. Stew, who prioritized product management, said, "There's no way we sold such a product. You must have mishandled it". The outraged woman left in anger, and her words profoundly impacted Stew. She said, "I came all the way from 12 miles away to tell you this. Fine! Before I die, I will never come back to this store again!"

Stew soon realized his mistake. He concluded that doubting a customer disqualified him from being in business. He resolved that all customer feedback is always right, with no exceptions, and decided to run the store according to the customers' needs, which led to the establishment of the Policy Stone.

Chapter

Service Customer

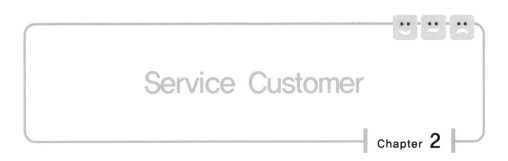

Service Customer

Chapter **2**

2.1 • Definition of a Customer

(1) Concept of a Customer

In a narrow sense, a customer refers simply to someone who buys or uses our products and services. In a broader sense, a customer includes everyone involved in the entire process of producing, using, and providing services, except for oneself. In other words, in modern society, everyone other than oneself can be considered a customer.

2.2 • Scope of Customers

(1) Overview

From a business perspective, generating profit is the ultimate goal, and since profits ultimately come from customers, managing customers effectively is crucial.

However, it is not possible to treat all customers uniformly due to their diverse and varied nature. Therefore, clearly defining different categories of customers and providing specialized services tailored to each customer's characteristics is a major aspect of business management.

(2) Classification

① Classification by Company Profit

a. Potential Customers: Customers who are either unaware of the company or aware but have not yet engaged in any transactions.

b. Prospective Customers: Customers who are aware of the company and show some level of interest, potentially becoming new customers.

c. New Customers: Customers who have just started doing business with the company for the first time.

d. Existing Customers: Customers who have an ongoing relationship with the company, allowing for accumulated customer data that facilitates efficient marketing and repeat purchases.

e. Loyal Customers: The most desirable type of customer for companies. These customers have a high level of loyalty to the company and consistently think of the company first when making a purchase, even without separate communication. They may also engage in word-of-mouth promotion.

② Classification Based on Customer Behavior Outcomes

a. Prospective Customers: All individuals who have the ability to purchase the company's products.

b. Potential Customers: Individuals who may need the company's products and have the purchasing power, and who already have information about the company's products.

c. Non—Qualified Potential Customers: Among the potential buyers, those who, like employees of competing companies, do not feel a need for the company's products or are definitely judged not to have the purchasing ability.

d. Repeat Customers: Consumers who have purchased the company's products at least twice.

e. Regular Customers: Consumers who maintain an ongoing relationship with the company and are not easily swayed by new strategies from competitors.

f. Advocate Customers: Regular customers who actively promote the company's products to others through word-of-mouth.

g. Inactive Customers: Former customers who have not engaged in any transactions with the company for a certain period of time

③ Classification Based on Process Perspective

a. Internal Customers

Individuals who use the results of the work performed by the person, such as colleagues and subordinates.

Customers (employees) who directly participate in value creation.

b. Intermediate Customers

Customers who deliver value between the company and the end consumers. Includes retailers, wholesalers, intermediaries, etc.

c. External Customers

Customers who use (consume) the value produced by the company. The end consumers or buyers of the final product.

④ Classification Based on Participation Perspective

a. Direct Customer (Primary Customer): Individuals who purchase products or services directly from the provider.

b. Indirect Customer (Individuals or Groups): End consumers or secondary consumers involved in indirect transactions.

c. Supplier Group: Entities that provide products and services and receive payment in return.

d. Internal Customer: Employees within the company, their families, and shareholders.

e. Decision-Making Customer: Individuals or groups that significantly influence the choices of direct customers (primary customers) but do not directly make purchases or pay money.

f. Opinion-Leading Customer: Groups that impact the reputation, reviews, and monitoring of products or services, rather than making purchases themselves (example: consumer protection organizations, journalists, critics, experts).

g. Regulatory Authorities: Legislators or government bodies that create laws applicable to consumer protection or related organizations.

h. Competitor: Individuals or groups (companies) that offer similar products or services, posing a threat to the company and increasing the need for strategic planning and customer management.

i. Regular Customer: Customers who repeatedly and consistently use the company's products or services but do not have enough loyalty to recommend the company to others.

j. Advocate Customer: Regular customers who have enough loyalty to actively recommend the company's products or services to others.

k. Marginal Customer: Customers whose activities or value negatively impact the company's profit, requiring exclusion from the customer list or inducement to terminate their engagement.

l. Cherry Picker: Customers who take advantage of special events or promotions to enjoy benefits but then do not engage with the company afterward. These customers typically do not make regular purchases or use services but exploit weaknesses in the company's service system or distribution structure to their own advantage.

⑤ Categories of Customers from a Contemporary Marketing Perspective

a. Consumer: The individual who ultimately uses the goods or services.

b. Buyer: The person who purchases the goods.

c. Purchasing Approver: The person who authorizes and approves the purchase.

d. Purchasing Influencer: The person who directly or indirectly influences the decision-making process regarding the purchase.

⑥ Gregory Stone's Customer Classification

In 1954, Gregory Stone proposed that even within the same organization or medical institution, customers can be classified into various types based on their perspectives and roles. This classification helps in understanding the attributes of different customers and allows for the development of appropriate marketing strategies to maximize customer satisfaction.

Economic Customer (Saver Customer)	• Customers seeking to maximize value • Customers who aim to get the highest utility from the time, money, and effort they invest • Customers who often verify the economic strengths of various service companies and closely examine their value, and who can sometimes be fickle
Ethical Customer (Moral Customer)	• Believes it is the customer's responsibility to support ethical companies. • Companies must maintain a clean and ethical social image to retain customers.
Personal Customer (Customization– Seeking Customer)	• Customers prefer personal interactions. • Customers desire services that recognize them personally over formal services. • With the recent trend toward personalization, marketing is possible if customer information is well utilized.
Convenience Customer	• Customers value convenience in the services they receive. • Customers are willing to pay extra for convenience.

2.3 ⊷ Customer Characteristics

(1) Understanding Customer Needs

① Maslow's Hierarchy of Needs[5]

When comparing Maslow's Hierarchy of Needs to service needs, it is as follows.

Physiologic al Needs	The basic needs for survival, such as food, clothing, and shelter	Is it provided in sufficient quantity at a reasonable price?
Safety Needs	The desire to be protected and safe from physical and emotional danger	Are the vegetables organic? Is the pork domestically sourced? Is the parking lot safe and convenient?
Love and Belonging Needs	As social beings, the need to belong to an organization, to have fellowship with colleagues, and to seek relationships or marriage	Are the employees friendly? Do they respond well to requests?
Esteem Needs	The desire to achieve self-esteem and autonomy (internal esteem needs) and to gain recognition from others and secure a certain status within a group (external esteem needs)	Do they show interest in me?
Self—Actuali zation Needs	The need to grow continuously through self-development, maximize one's potential, and achieve self-actualization	Do they recognize me and provide better service than they do to others?

② Basic Customer Needs

    a. Customers want to be remembered.

    b. They want to feel welcomed and be given attention.

    c. They want to be recognized as important individuals.

---

5) Maslow, A. H. (1943). A theory of human motivation. *Psychological review, 50*(4), 370-396.

d. They seek comfort.

e. They desire to be praised.

f. They expect and want their expectations and demands to be met.

③ Main Characteristics

a. The customer is king and always right.

b. Customers have many demands and strong assertions of their rights.

c. Even if it is a mistake by one out of 1,000 employees, from the customer's perspective, it is a 100% mistake.

d. Customers can be fickle and may change their purchasing source at any time.

e. Do not fully trust what customers say; they may praise you to your face but criticize you behind your back.

f. Listening to customers' complaints can turn them into loyal customers.

g. It is more concerning when customers do not express their dissatisfaction.

h. Customers weigh whether the service they received matches the amount they paid.

I. Customers like prompt and accurate service.

j. Customers want to be recognized as individuals.

k. Customers can be impulsive.

l. Customers are very sensitive to first impressions.

④ Understanding Customer Characteristics

The most necessary skills for understanding customer characteristics are insight and analytical ability. Insight is the ability to penetrate the essence, while analytical ability is fundamental for creating new items.

a. Be sensitive to customer changes.

Customers are always changing, so tailored strategies to respond to these changes are necessary. For example, when Home Depot noticed that their main customer base was aging and losing interest in the DIY home renovation section, they developed an installation service business, which became a great success.

b. Observe and confirm by direct contact with customers.

It is essential to observe the needs of customers and produce products that match these needs. For instance, Sony realized that their gaming consoles were too complicated for parents and that children faced disapproval from their parents while playing. This led to a decline in demand for their consoles. In response, they developed the Nintendo, an easy-to-use gaming console that parents and children could enjoy together, making them a leader in the gaming industry.

c. Value customer touchpoints.

It is crucial to provide the best service at the moment of contact with the customer.

(2) Customer DNA

① Significance

Customer DNA refers to a broad range of customer information. Customer DNA can be broadly categorized into three main types, with the most important being information about customer needs and preferences.

Demographic DNA	• Customer Profile DNA: Includes information such as name, address (postal, email), phone number (home, office, mobile, fax), workplace, department, position (promotion date), alma mater, and anniversaries (birthdays, wedding anniversaries, company founding dates), etc. • Relationship DNA: Includes family relationships, close friends, community memberships (community members and main profiles), and referral information (customers who referred them), etc.
Customer Value DNA	• Customer Classification Grade: Your own customer classification criteria (e.g., classified into five grades: S, A, B, C, D). • Contract Information: Product name, timing, frequency and number of purchases, amount, customer lifetime value (LTV: Life Time Value), and customer wallet share. • Purchasing Power Information: Income level and sources of income, income change trends, and asset status.
Customer Needs and Preferences DNA	• Customer Needs DNA: Needs related to products (preferred brands or products, designs, colors, etc.). • Customer Preferences and Dispositions DNA: Hobbies, specialties (ways of enjoying hobbies/joined clubs), preferences (alcohol, tobacco, food, clothing), personality, communication style, decision-making style, cultural and artistic inclinations, etc.

② Identifying and Managing Customer DNA

To turn a person into a customer, it is necessary to meet them several times and collect customer DNA information during each interaction. To achieve this, a customer DNA information file should be created, such as the individual customer notebook used by Nordstrom. Additionally, a list of DNA information to be identified during each customer meeting should be prepared and updated continuously every day without fail. This effort should be applied equally to existing customers as well.

CRM (Customer Relationship Management)

CRM (Customer Relationship
Management)

3.1 Overview of CRM

(1) Concept

① Significance

Customer Relationship Management (CRM) is defined as a management technique that involves planning and executing marketing strategies tailored to individual customer characteristics by analyzing customer needs and behaviors. This is based on customer support systems such as customer consultation applications, customer databases, and contact management systems, with the goal of acquiring new customers and retaining existing ones.

② Features

a. Discovering what customers want and providing it in the desired way at the desired time.

b. Placing more emphasis on customer retention rather than customer acquisition.

c. Focusing on improving relationships to become closer to customers.

d. Managing customers' lifestyle patterns.

③ Objectives of CRM

The goal of CRM is to enhance company profitability and reduce costs by optimizing customer value. Specifically, the objectives are:

a. To focus on increasing customer numbers through the acquisition of new customers and retention of existing ones, prioritizing customer share over market share.

b. To improve sales and customer loyalty through the enhancement of customer value.

c. To reduce costs by improving the efficiency of customer operational expenses.

d. To increase company profitability and reduce costs by optimizing customer retention expenses and improving the efficiency of marketing expenditures.

④ Research Findings Highlighting the Importance of CRM

a. 65% of company revenue comes from satisfied customers.

b. The cost of acquiring new customers is approximately five times greater than the cost of retaining existing customers.

c. The revenue generated by the top 20% of customers is comparable to that generated by the remaining 80% of customers.

d. Most companies lose about 15% to 20% of their customers annually.

e. Even a slight increase in customer retention rates can boost profits by 25% to 100%.

f. Less than 10% of dissatisfied customers contact the company to express their complaints.

g. 91% of unsatisfied customers will never purchase from the company again and will share their negative experiences with at least nine people.

⑤ Importance of CRM

a. Emphasizes customer share over market share.

b. Focuses on customer retention rather than customer acquisition.

c. Prioritizes customer relationships over product sales.

d. Efforts are concentrated on customer relationships within target markets and target customers.

e. Builds long-term and deep trust relationships with customers to prevent existing customers from leaving.

(2) Areas of CRM

① Customer Retention

As a primary focus area of relationship marketing, it requires both passive and active efforts.

- Passive Efforts: Preventing customer complaints and effectively addressing them when they arise.

- Active Efforts: Providing additional benefits before customers even make a request.

② Customer Acquisition

Customer acquisition refers to the process of securing new customers by utilizing external databases. This involves identifying the characteristics of high-value customers through retention activities and, based on these results, prioritizing individuals with potential to become high-value customers as new clients.

a. MGM (Member Get Member): This method involves acquiring new customers through existing customers. It was initiated with the aim of attracting new customers from the perspective of existing partners. Essentially, marketing activities are conducted using information about potential new customers provided by existing ones.

b. Partnership Method: This involves sharing information through formal partnerships between companies. Partnerships are established with the goal of information sharing, and companies with relevant information carry out marketing activities.

③ Customer Development

Customer development refers to the efforts to continuously increase the value of already acquired customers.

a. Cross-Selling: Activities aimed at encouraging customers to purchase new products beyond their existing purchases.

b. Up-Selling: Activities designed to increase the purchase amount within a specific category of products.

(3) Background of CRM Emergence

① Changes in Customers

The intense market competition of the late 1990s and the advent of the internet made it possible for customers to switch to competitors at any time if they chose to, generating diverse and personalized expectations and demands from customers. As a result, companies adopted CRM (Customer Relationship Management), a customer-centric management approach, to meet changing customer expectations and demands, maintain stable customer relationships, and sustain their competitive advantage.

② Changes in the Market

Since the late 1990s, market deregulation, increased competition, market maturation, economic downturns, and diversification of sales channels have led to a rise in supply over demand. This shift transformed the market from being producer-centered to buyer-centered. In a buyer-centered market, customers seek products and services that match their individual preferences and desires, significantly diminishing the effectiveness of mass marketing, which treats customers as a homogeneous group. Consequently, companies adopted CRM (Customer Relationship Management), a customer-marketing approach that involves setting target customers based on strategic customer segmentation and implementing appropriate marketing mixes.

③ Advancements in Information Technology (IT)

Rapid advancements in computer hardware storage capacity and data processing performance have enabled companies to store vast amounts of customer-related data in data warehouses and perform scientific customer analysis using techniques such as data mining. These IT developments not only provided companies with crucial information and insights about customers and markets but also created a technological environment conducive to the adoption of CRM.

④ Changes in Marketing Communication

As market segmentation increased due to customer diversity, traditional mass media broadcasting advertisements became less effective. To enhance advertising efficiency, it is essential to first establish specific advertising goals, identify target customers, and then engage in differentiated target marketing that addresses their needs and desires. Moving away from merely informing customers about products or services, the focus is now on maintaining long-term relationships with customers, which is a key strategy to improve advertising effectiveness.

(4) Expected Benefits of CRM

① Marketing Aspect

a. Increase in Revenue and Customer Lifetime Value: By attracting new customers and revitalizing existing ones to create lifelong customer relationships, CRM can enhance revenue and customer lifetime value.

b. Effective Marketing at Critical Points: CRM enables effective marketing activities at decisive moments in the customer lifecycle.

c. Capturing New Market Opportunities: Through trust-based information exchange with customers, CRM is useful for identifying new market opportunities.

② Effects from a business Aspect

a. The company can quickly grasp and respond to changes in customer needs, allowing for the development of products that match changes in market and customer needs.

b. It enables targeted marketing by classifying highly profitable customers.

c. It allows for quick response to seize opportunities in niche markets.

③ Customer Service Aspect

a. Increasing Customer Satisfaction: By understanding customer behavior, CRM enhances customer satisfaction, which ultimately improves customer loyalty and retention rates.

b. Boosting Sales: CRM creates opportunities for repeat purchases, cross-selling, and up-selling, leading to increased sales.

④ Channel Management Aspect

Guide customers to channels that best fit their needs and minimize costs.

(5) Building and Implementing a Successful CRM

① Significance of CRM Construction

The overall CRM process can be summarized into three main phases: strategy formulation, system construction, and execution. Among these, the strategy formulation and system construction phases are considered the CRM construction stages. In these CRM construction stages, the most critical task is finding answers to how the CRM techniques can be utilized to provide more value to customers compared to competitors. This is what constitutes the CRM strategy. The CRM strategy is akin to the framework of the entire CRM system. Therefore, if the strategy is weak, even the best system will struggle to achieve successful outcomes.

② Prerequisites for CRM Construction

a. Establishment of a Unified Customer Database: Integrate data related to customers, products, and transactions based on a data warehouse perspective. In other words, a CRM system requires the establishment of a company-wide information sharing system related to customers.

b. Data Mining Tools for Analyzing Customer Characteristics: Use data mining tools on the established unified customer database to analyze customer traits and behaviors.

c. Campaign Management Tools for Marketing Activities: Analyze the characteristics of individual customers who have been classified to prepare for marketing campaigns.

③ CRM Construction Process

a. Data Collection: This involves gathering both internal and external data related to the company.

- Data: Includes customer attribute information obtained during transactions, transaction-related data, accounting information, credit evaluation data, partnership utilization data, etc.

b. Data Refining: This step involves removing anomalies and duplicates from the data. Special attention is given to verifying missing data and erroneous data.

c. Building a Data Warehouse: Essential for continuous customer management. Frequently analyzed data is managed as a data mart. If budget constraints make it difficult to maintain a data warehouse, operating only a data mart can be considered.

d. Customer Analysis and Data Mining: Predict customer behavior and measure profitability and value based on the analysis of customer preferences and demands.

e. Integration with Marketing Channels: Use the analyzed results in sales or customer service departments to support marketing activities.

f. Utilization of Feedback Information: Evaluate the results of marketing activities and use meaningful information as marketing data for future improvements.

| CRM Construction Process |

Data Collection → Data Refining → Building a Data Warehouse → Customer Analysis and
Data Mining → Integration with Marketing Channels → Utilization of Feedback
Information

④ 6 Steps to Establishing a CRM Strategy

• Step 1: Environmental Analysis

Environmental analysis involves designing precise objectives for CRM and
analyzing the market environment to respond appropriately to customers
before implementing CRM. Since the ultimate goal of CRM is to secure
loyal customers and convert them into profitable ones through long-term
relationships, it is crucial to analyze various aspects: the internal processes
of the company from a customer-centric perspective, customer responses to
external market changes, customer satisfaction with the company's products,
and competitors' customer strategies.

• Step 2: Customer Analysis

After identifying market trends and the flow of numerous unspecified
customers through market analysis, customer analysis focuses on examining
the company's current customer base from multiple angles. This analysis
involves understanding how the existing customers are composed and includes
customer evaluation for profitability conversion and customer segmentation
to build long-term relationships and secure loyal customers.

• Step 3: Setting CRM Strategy Direction

Setting the CRM strategy direction involves determining what the company
aims to achieve with CRM, how it will be implemented, and the expected

effects. This step seeks to find ways to enhance business performance by differentiating customer services from competitors. The strategy direction should ultimately help in reducing marketing costs and maximizing company revenue. To increase revenue, companies need to develop strategies to secure customers and continuously build relationships with existing ones to capture their lifetime value. Companies should use various marketing activities, such as events, campaigns, partnerships, and promotions, to acquire customers and improve relationships. Additionally, leveraging customer data for customer service responses, increasing purchase amounts through upselling, or encouraging cross-selling of different products can be effective. Reducing marketing costs involves integrating customer data to save unnecessary resources, efficiently utilizing data for marketing decisions, and implementing cost-effective marketing campaigns to maintain ongoing relationships and convert customers into loyal ones.

- Step 4: Determining Customer Offers

Based on customer membership information, various interactions with customers, and transaction history, determine marketing offers tailored to customer characteristics such as product interests, income levels, transaction frequency, and average purchase amount.

- Step 5: Personalization Design

To design personalization, analyze personal information such as gender, age, occupation, and income, as well as purchase-related data including product types, purchase prices, purchase frequency, and webpage content interests. The goal is to create personalized rules that foster ongoing, interactive communication between the company and customers, rather than just providing formalized products or information.

Step 6: Communication Design

Once the service to be provided is determined, design the method of delivery. This could involve internet-based methods (such as email, text messages, and web content) or traditional methods (such as mail, phone calls, and face-to-face interactions). Effective communication also requires attention to aspects like presentation and packaging.

Expression	• Efforts are needed to differentiate the expression of messages according to the customer's personal characteristics. • The content should be adjusted to match the customer's level of understanding. • The core message should be clearly emphasized. • Messages should be delivered in a way that fosters maximum empathy with the customer.
Packaging	• A special packaging that allows the content to be viewed at once is necessary. • Mail: The packaging should convey the feeling that there is something special inside. • Email: Attention should be captured with emphasized formatting, beautiful graphics, and unique backgrounds.

3.2 CRM Successful Analysis

(1) CRM Successful Analysis

① Strategies by Customer Type

a. Potential Customers (or New Prospects): Strategy for acquiring new customers

b. New Customers and General Customers: Strategy for strengthening relationships

c. At-Risk Customers: Strategy for preventing churn and strengthening relationships

d. High-Value Customers: Strategy for maintaining high-value status

e. Regular Customers and Poor-Performing Customers: Strategy for improving to high-value status

f. Former Customers: Strategy for re-engagement

② Customer Acquisition Strategy

This strategy aims to convert potential customers who have never purchased from the company into buyers of its products. It involves acquiring new customer lists through methods such as surveys, direct response advertisments, promotions, and using data from other companies' customer databases.

a. Criteria for Analyzing Potential Customers

b. Strategies for Identifying Potential Customers

- Attempt contact with customers using customer data

- Household Analysis: Identify targets with similar characteristics to current customers

c. Strategies for Converting to New Customers

- Provide product samples, advertising materials, and discount coupons to potential customers
- Offer gifts or discount benefits to existing customers

③ Customer Retention Strategy

Durable goods, such as home appliances and automobiles, tend to be relatively expensive and carry significant social imagery, leading to high perceived risk and involvement from the customer's perspective. As a result, customers may feel anxious about whether their purchase decision was the right one. The customer retention strategy aims to alleviate this anxiety by providing various forms of information about the purchased product (such as after-sales service, product usage instructions, compatible accessories, and positive product reviews) and expressing personal attention to the customer who made the purchase. This helps to foster a favorable attitude towards the product and reinforces the customer's satisfaction with their purchase.

* Customer Retention Strategy Approaches
  - Establish a System for Managing Customer Complaints and Develop Solutions
  - Predicting Potential Churn: Use data mining techniques to analyze customers' demographic data and transaction patterns to predict the likelihood of customer churn
  - Develop Models for Analyzing Poor-Performing Customers
  - Compensation Strategies for Customers

• Strategies to Enhance Customer Profitability

④ Customer Activation Strategy

This strategy aims to increase the frequency of purchases by continuously recording transactions with customers and offering sales promotions such as incentives, sampling, coupons, and giveaways based on purchase volume. For consumers with relatively high purchase frequency, customer activation strategies should focus on enhancing brand loyalty and increasing the frequency of product use.

⑤ Loyalty Enhancement Strategy

The core of this strategy is to strengthen relationships with fixed customers by enhancing services, thereby preventing them from switching to competitors' products and increasing their loyalty to the company's products.

⑥ Cross-Selling Strategy

In cases where a company offers a variety of products, the cross-selling strategy involves encouraging customers who have purchased one product to buy additional products. This is done by using the existing product database to promote new products. For example, information about a 30-year-old woman who bought kitchenware like pots at a department store can be used to implement cross-selling strategies for other kitchen items or appliances. Similarly, financial institutions can analyze the characteristics of customers who already hold their financial products and use this analysis to design programs that encourage these customers to purchase additional financial products that have the highest likelihood of appeal.

• Cross-Selling: Integrating and selling other products that customers are likely to be interested in, within the existing product line.

• Upselling: Encouraging customers to purchase upgrades when their current equipment is worn out or requires replacement.

For example, an internet company might offer a program where customers can replace their existing modem with a more advanced one by paying a small additional fee.

⑦ Customer Reactivation Strategy

Customers who have previously purchased goods or services are generally more likely to be converted into valuable customers compared to those with no prior transaction history. To reactivate past customers, it is crucial to maintain and manage a database of former customers. This involves a thorough analysis of past performance and identifying appropriate reasons for why the transactions ceased.

⑧ Specific Methods for Enhancing CRM Capabilities

a. Building Trust with Customers

b. Maintaining Long-Term Relationships Over Short-Term Gains

c. Strong Commitment from Management

d. Establishing a Collaborative System Among Relevant Departments

e. Fair and Equitable Treatment

f. Open Channels for Communication

(2) Customer Relationship Management Activity Model

① prospective customer search activity

a. CRM starts with prospecting for potential customers. Here, prospects are defined as customers who present a sales opportunity.

b. Prospecting activities involve the continuous process of identifying customers who are likely to use the company's products and services.

c. To effectively prospect, it is important to clearly define target customers.

d. Identify customers with purchasing motives, register them in a prospect registration center, and use direct marketing methods such as Direct Mail (DM), Telemarketing (TM), and email to assess customer response and transaction potential.

e. Establish a 1:1 communication system with customers by registering store visit information, encouraging customer referrals, having staff introduce customers, partnering with external related companies, or discovering prospects through the web. Create a standard process for collecting and utilizing customer information across all touchpoint channels.

② New Customer Acquisition Activities

a. New customer acquisition involves closely engaging with prospects who present a sales opportunity until they make a purchase.

b. Sales is not just about selling products; it is about delivering the value of the company.

c. The process for acquiring new customers primarily involves activities such as Direct Mail (DM), Telemarketing (TM), email, and in-person visits. It includes both sales activities driven by customer requests and proactive sales efforts.

d. To increase the likelihood of sales, sales representatives must identify which customers are strategically valuable among many. They should understand what products and services the customer desires and what the key purchasing factors are, then approach the customer with solutions that address their needs.

e. To maintain a good relationship and ongoing communication with customers, it is important to effectively manage the customer information obtained during the consultation process.

③ New Customer Management Activities

a. Understanding the key reasons for new customers' purchases is crucial.

b. Implement a formal 'Welcome Program'.

c. During the first 3 months, it is important to observe the behavior and attitudes of new customers, and it is beneficial to build relationship experiences with them at least twice within this period.

④ Customer Information Collection and Understanding Activities

It is necessary to gather information about customer attitudes and strategically identify potential future high-value customers.

⑤ Customer Value Enhancement Activities

a. This involves the ongoing process of providing continuous value to customers.

b. To enhance customer value, implement Cross-selling, Up-selling, and Re-selling campaigns, and strategically reallocate marketing resources to focus on growth potential customer segments.

c. Maintain close 1:1 relationships with target customers and implement intensive Cross-selling and Up-selling strategies for growth potential customer groups.

d. Cross-Selling/Up-Selling Programs

• Definition: Activities that enhance customer value and increase company profitability by offering utilities (products or services) that customers have not previously experienced.

- Objective: Increase sales through enhanced customer value and secure a stable revenue base by retaining existing customers.
- Program Examples: In the case of home shopping companies, use association analysis of products purchased by customers to display related products nearby and develop additional promotional items.

⑥ Premium Customer Management Activities

a. Premium customers seek differentiated services, so it is important to recognize them as valuable and provide tailored management solutions.

b. Premium Customer Management Program

- Definition: Offering differentiated services to high-value customers to enhance their loyalty to the company.
- Objective: Increase profitability through deeper customer relationships and encourage customers to become voluntary advocates for the company. While improving satisfaction among premium customers is effective, it is also crucial to motivate other customers to aspire to become premium customers.
- Examples of Premium Programs: Free parking on weekends and holidays, dedicated account managers for premium customers, free legal and tax consultations, and exclusive service counters for premium customers.

⑦ Customer Complaint Management Activities

a. Analyze the root causes of complaints to understand the underlying issues.

b. Customers who express complaints have the potential to become loyal customers. View complaints as opportunities to impress and engage customers, and respond actively to address their concerns.

⑧ Customer Retention Activities

    a. These activities involve identifying dormant customers or those likely to churn in advance and taking measures to prevent their defection.

    b. Regular contact management with customers is crucial for preventing churn. It is important to manage not only dissatisfied customers but also indifferent customers.

    c. Customer Retention Program

        • Definition: A series of activities aimed at preventing the defection of valuable customers by understanding customer churn using information on existing defectors.

        • Purpose: To prevent revenue loss, minimize customer acquisition and management costs, and avoid damaging the company's image due to the spread of dissatisfaction by unhappy customers.

        • Program Examples: Providing events and discount benefits

⑨ Customer Reacquisition Activities

The key to reacquiring former customers is to focus on those who were previously highly profitable. Implementing a 'Welcome Program' for reacquired customers is essential to successfully bringing them back.

| Customer Management Activity Model (9 Steps of Customer Relationship Management) |

New Customer Acquisition	1. Prospecting Activities ↓ 2. New Customer Acquisition Activities
Customer Value Enhancement	↓ 3. New Customer Management Activities ↓ 4. Customer Information Collection and Understanding Activities ↓ 5. Customer Value Enhancement Activities ↓
Customer Retention	6. Premium Customer Management Activities ↓ 7. Customer Complaint Management Activities ↓ 8. Customer Retention Activities ↓ 9. Reacquisition of Former Customers Activities

(3) CRM Cases of Companies by Industry

① Cheil Industries (Chemicals)

Cheil Industries discovered through customer data analysis that the top 20% of their customers contribute 63% of the total customer revenue, while the top 40% account for approximately 80% of the total revenue. This indicates that high-revenue customers have a relatively significant impact. Based on these findings, since the year 2000, Cheil Industries has implemented targeted marketing by classifying customers into four major categories.

General Customers	Data on customers with experience purchasing from Cheil Industries
Premium Customers	Customers who have purchased Cheil Industries products 3 or more times: Total of 170,000 people. They receive a fashion information magazine from Cheil Industries issued quarterly.
VIP Customers	Customers who have purchased 5 or more times: Approximately 50,000 people. They receive free repairs for Cheil Industries products, an exclusive VIP hotline for resolving inconveniences, and a gift voucher worth 30,000 won.
Royal Customers	Customers who have purchased 5 or more times with a total expenditure of over 5 million won: Approximately 20,000 people. They are issued a separate membership card that offers 7% reward points on purchases (compared to the standard 5%). Additionally, they receive birthday flower delivery and are invited to two exclusive Royal Service Days per year.

Additionally, starting from January 2002, the company implemented a 1:1 communication system called "Fassenger", a blend of "Fashion" and "Messenger". This system informs customers about special occasions such as birthdays and anniversaries via text messages and emails. Targeted at loyal customers, Fassenger is designed to maintain high-value customers and stimulate repeat purchases through personalized marketing activities based on fundamental data of fixed customers.

A notable feature of this system is the provision of messages in each store, where data on customer sizes and purchasing characteristics are managed and direct marketing is carried out. Cheil Industries sent a total of 1.4 million messages to customers. Before the implementation of this system in 2001, the number of loyal customers was 870,000; by 2002, it had increased to 2.26 million, marking a 193% growth. This shows a positive response in terms of customer management.

② HP Inc.

HP Inc. needed to lay the groundwork for building an e-Relationship and securing customer information through the web and email. However, since HP primarily sold products through wholesalers and not directly, the company did not have direct access to customer information. This situation necessitated not only the creation of a new email database from scratch but also the development of an entirely new email system. HP's email marketing team faced the challenge of organizing a vast amount of customer database information handed over by various channel managers. Furthermore, HP's customers were divided into general consumers and IT companies, each with entirely different interests and preferences. This division was problematic for email marketing, where personalization and customization are crucial. Consequently, HP pursued various strategic goals to ensure the success of their CRM system.

Strategically, HP decided to focus overall marketing efforts on email marketing and devised all preparatory steps needed to achieve this goal. They conducted internal and external surveys to determine optimal messaging times, understanding that customers have varying preferences for when they want to receive information and that customers prefer to take the lead in their relationships with companies. They also identified how to enhance customer profiles by analyzing website visitor usage. Based on these findings, they began designing their email system.

HP hired an external firm, Digital Impact, to build the email system. Finally, HP needed to create an email database and systematically collected as many email addresses as possible to establish their corporate email system. This specialized CRM system generated $300 million in revenue annually through

HP's email marketing efforts and reduced the website's membership cancellation rate to nearly zero. Moreover, there were no complaints about spam emails from customers due to their effective email marketing approach.

3.3 CRM Failure Analysis

(1) Overview

Since customers are what bring profits to a company, how a company manages its customers can significantly impact its competitiveness. Therefore, many companies have actively adopted and implemented CRM, investing time and research into it, but they often fail to achieve the desired results. Although CRM seems promising in terms of generating profits, there are many cases of failure. Let's examine the issues through the following failure cases.

(2) Case Study

① Financial Institution

A financial institution once attempted a direct mail (DM) campaign to promote student loans targeting farming households at the start of a new academic year. At that time, many rural families were sending their children to universities in cities, so the campaign was designed to target these households for student loan sales. However, the campaign was planned without sufficient information about the customers and was executed as a pilot program without prior testing. This led to unexpected results and the campaign was classified as a failure.

The campaign involved sending direct mail to about 10,000 farming households in the area, requesting them to visit a branch with the necessary documents to apply for student loans. The mail also promised special interest rates and differentiated services to encourage visits. However, when these farming households visited the branch with the requested documents, most were denied loan approval.

The reason given by the loan assessment team was that many of these farmers already had significant debt from long-term low-interest agricultural loans from the government. Therefore, additional student loans would increase their debt burden, making approval impossible. As a result, the student loan campaign ended in complete failure, leading to direct complaints and dissatisfaction from customers who were unable to secure loans, as well as negative word-of-mouth spread. The campaign turned out to be a worse sales activity than not conducting it at all.

② Telecom Company

A telecom company, referred to as Company A, faced a significant drop in market share in strategically important regions compared to its competitors. To address this issue, the company decided to launch an aggressive telemarketing (TM) campaign with a special offer: their long-distance or international call rates were 15% lower than those of competitors.

Initially, the company targeted specific customer segments in these competitive regions to improve efficiency through targeted marketing. However, contrary to expectations, the response from these selected customers was lukewarm, and the campaign failed to achieve its goals. Under continued pressure from management to resolve the market share decline, the marketing team expanded the telemarketing efforts to include former customers and potential customers. Despite this broader approach, the response rate still did not meet expectations. Unable to withstand further pressure from management, the marketing team expanded the target audience once again, leading to a situation where the campaign effectively became mass marketing aimed at over half of the customers in the region. This shift from a carefully selected target audience to a broad mass marketing approach resulted in the failure of the market share recovery efforts and, similarly to traditional mass marketing experiences, led to significant waste of both time and resources.

(3) Conclusion and Future Directions

① Reasons and Issues of CRM Implementation Failure

Despite the numerous CRM projects conducted, there are few cases where practical results have been achieved. The concept of CRM itself is quite rational, so it's not that CRM is inherently flawed. So, is the problem that CRM performance takes a long time to manifest, or is it that the implementation and execution of CRM are flawed?

To conclude, both are correct. Firstly, excessive expectations from CRM are problematic. While CRM is indeed a necessary activity, it is important not to harbor illusions about its effectiveness. To enhance management performance through CRM, one must first set realistic performance expectations for CRM. Additionally, without a clear understanding of what the company can gain from CRM, failure is likely. Even the best tools are meaningless if not implemented suitably for the company's situation, and CRM is not needed by every industry or company. Furthermore, even if a company needs CRM, success will only be possible if a clear understanding of CRM's characteristics and functions precedes the introduction of an appropriate CRM system.

The inadequacy of customer data also plays a significant role in the failure to achieve desired CRM results. Expecting success from CRM when there is either no data or erroneous data is impractical. Besides data issues, system-related problems can also be a cause. Since CRM is based on IT technology elements, inadequate system infrastructure can lead to CRM failure.

Successful CRM requires consideration of various factors. Besides the general problems mentioned, issues such as lack of collaboration between work teams and careless data management are also cited as obstacles to successful CRM. Ultimately, the problem often lies not in CRM and its implementation tools themselves but within the internal practices of the adopting company.

② Methods for Successful CRM Implementation

a. A clear strategy suitable for the company's situation must be established. It is not a matter of how advanced CRM technology is, but rather which technology is appropriate for the company that is important.

b. Rather than expecting immediate results from CRM, it is important to systematically implement CRM from a long-term perspective. If CRM is viewed as a one-time activity with visible results, performance measurement will inevitably be short-term, and such performance measurement will lead to CRM being regarded as an inconsequential management method. The performance of CRM should be measured from a long-term perspective through indicators such as customer retention rate, customer growth rate, and brand preference.

c. It is crucial to determine not only how to provide products to each customer but also what to provide. In CRM, providing information tailored to the characteristics of each customer is a key success factor. This requires in-depth analysis of customer information and high-quality data collection.

d. To ensure smooth interaction with customers, improving communication is essential. This necessitates the training and development of customer service representatives' skills.

3.4 ⟶ Relationship Marketing

(1) Definition of Relationship Marketing

① Microscopic Perspective Definition: Definition from the perspective of the interaction between the company and the customer (narrow definition of relationship marketing)

a. Berry (1983)[6]: Marketing activities aimed at creating, maintaining, and enhancing relationships with consumers.

b. Rapp & Collins (1990)[7]: Marketing efforts aimed at creating and maintaining a mutually beneficial and ongoing relationship between the company and the customer.

---

6) Berry, L. L. (1983). Relationship marketing. In L. L. Berry, G. L. Shostack, & G. Upah (Eds.), *Emerging perspectives on services marketing* (pp. 25-28). American Marketing Association.

7) Rapp, S., & Collins, T. (1990). *The great marketing turnaround.* Prentice Hall.

② Macroscopic Perspective Definition: Defined in terms of relationships with various business partners, including customers, employees, suppliers, competitors, and government entities, or defined with a focus on establishing a stable relationship structure with business partners.

a. Gronroos (1990)[8]: Maintaining and strengthening relationships with customers and partners to ensure that the goals of relevant stakeholders are met at the level of securing the company's profits.

b. Christopher (1991)[9]: Creating and enhancing relationships not only with customers but also with suppliers, employees, referrers, stakeholders, and the internal market.

c. Conclusion: Relationship marketing can be defined as marketing activities aimed at creating, maintaining, and strengthening long-term bonds with business partners such as customers, buyers, suppliers, and competitors, with the goal of increasing the company's profitability.

(2) Objectives of Relationship Marketing

The objectives of relationship marketing are to acquire new customers, retain existing customers, and strengthen customer relationships.

① Attraction of New Customers: When attracting new customers, companies segment the market based on customers' expectations, desires, and preferences. This allows them to identify the optimal target market for building sustainable customer relationships. To attract new customers,

---

8) Gronroos, C. (1990). Relationship approach to marketing in service contexts: The marketing and organizational behavior interface. *Journal of Business Research, 20*(1), 3-11.

9) Christopher, M., Payne, A., & Ballantyne, D. (1991). *Relationship marketing.* Heinemann.

companies use methods such as leveraging the word-of-mouth effect from existing customers and employing the Members Get Members (MGM) technique, which offers incentives to customers who recommend new ones.

② Retention of Existing Customers: While acquiring new customers is essential for business expansion, it is equally important to manage existing customers effectively. If a company understands and adapts to the changing needs of its customers and reflects these changes in its services, it can maintain ongoing customer relationships through repeat purchases driven by customer satisfaction.

③ Enhancement of Customer Relationships: As customers continue to be satisfied with a company's products or services over time, their relationship with the company strengthens, potentially turning them into loyal customers. The extent to which a company can secure loyal customers is a fundamental factor that reflects the company's foundation and growth potential. Strengthening relationships with customers improves the company's customer share, market share, and profit base.

(3) Characteristics of Relationship Marketing

① Focus on Retaining Existing Customers: Marketing strategies are centered on the maintenance and management of existing customers rather than acquiring new ones.

② Relationship marketing aims for profit generation through long-term relationships rather than short-term transactions, focusing on the long-term customer lifetime value rather than immediate sales results.

③ The focus of marketing shifts to the customer as the exchange entity, recognizing customers as partners in the business. Marketing strategies are directed towards product differentiation.

④ The goal of marketing is oriented towards forming, maintaining, and strengthening customer relationships rather than just achieving transactional outcomes.

⑤ Internal marketing and interactions at customer touchpoints are prioritized, with a focus on functional quality or process quality over technical quality.

⑥ The focus shifts from economies of scale to economies of scope, meaning the aim is to sell a range of products to a single customer or maintain long-term transactions with each customer.

⑦ Marketing performance indicators transition from market share to customer share.

⑧ Pursuing long-term customer relationships and loyalty leads to lower price sensitivity among consumers.

⑨ Competitors become partners in a competitive and cooperative relationship, working together as well as competing.

⑩ Internal marketing is seen as a prerequisite for effective external marketing.

⑪ There is a strong emphasis on two-way communication between the company and the customer, with a high value placed on customer service and customer engagement.

| Comparison of Mass Marketing and Relationship Marketing |

Category	Mass Marketing	Relationship Marketing
Source of Revenue	• Product • Developing and selling superior products leads to business growth	• Customer • The ability to respond to customers determines the fate of the business
Customer Approach	Carpet Bombing Strategy	Missile Strategy
Perspective on Sales Growth	Focus on market share	Focus on customer share
Performance Evaluation Perspective	Focus on short-term performance	Long-term performance focus

(4) Effects of Relationship Marketing

Successfully implementing relationship marketing can increase a company's profitability through enhanced customer loyalty, resulting word-of-mouth effects, and cost savings from operational efficiencies due to learning effects.

① Effects from the Company's Perspective

a. Achieves cost-effectiveness in customer retention through long-term customer relationships.

b. Enhances customer value by involving customers in the customization of offerings and production processes.

c. Enables new market segmentation strategies based on customer relationships.

d. Secures a competitive advantage through 1:1 marketing based on customer databases.

e. Utilizes long-term customer relationships for cross-selling or cross-promotion, reducing wasteful promotion costs associated with mass media.

f. Strengthens long-term relationships and builds barriers to switching competitors by increasing trust, customer loyalty, and engagement in customer relationships.

② Effects from the Market Perspective

a. Accumulates information and knowledge about customers to provide personalized offerings.

b. Maximizes perceived value and relationship value by individualizing customer relationships.

c. Increases the efficiency of customer decision-making and reduces perceived risk.

d. Secures customer loyalty and a stable revenue base, while gaining positive word-of-mouth effects.

e. Builds strong ties with relationship partners, which become a source of competitive advantage.

③ Effects from the Competitive Perspective

a. Reduces risks and costs through horizontal collaborations such as strategic alliances.

b. Achieves economies of scale, production rationalization, cost savings through inter-firm comparative advantages, joint research and development, and technological synergy through corporate cooperation.

c. Enhances economies of speed, including shortening new product introduction times, quickly securing new technologies and markets, gaining first-mover advantages, and improving market response times.

d. Effectively manages competitive and co-dependent interrelationships and uncertainties within the industry.

e. Establishes a horizontal collaboration structure as a source of competitive advantage.

3.5 e-CRM

(1) Definition

e-CRM refers to the process of collecting and analyzing customer data gathered online to identify valuable customers. It involves prioritizing the investment of the company's limited resources in acquiring and retaining these valuable customers.

(2) Background for the Emergence of e-CRM

① The importance of traditional CRM operations was highlighted in the context of e-business.

② The limitations of traditional CRM, such as constraints of time and place, and the diversification of channels, became evident as the business environment evolved.

(3) Objectives of e-CRM

① Respond quickly to customer demands through the internet

② Enhance the ability to predict customer behavior, leading to increased customer satisfaction (and loyalty)

③ Ultimately increase the company's revenue

(4) Components of e-CRM

① Operational CRM

a. Operational CRM is a system that supports concrete execution and primarily focuses on the functions of the front office.

b. It is a system that supports the enhancement of relationships between the organization and its customers, specifically aiding the organization's comprehensive operations.

c. Specific examples include Contact Management functions and Sales Force Automation (SFA) functions.

② Analytical CRM

a. Analytical CRM is focused on the back office and is centered around analyzing customer information based on a data warehouse to support marketing activities.

b. It is a system that extracts and analyzes customer data to utilize it in sales, marketing, and service aspects.

c. Through this, opportunities and ideas for customer and market segmentation, customer profiling, discovering product concepts, campaign management, event planning, and promotion planning can be derived.

③ Collaborative CRM

Collaborative CRM refers to the integration of analysis and operational systems and includes various customer touchpoint tools designed to facilitate interactions between customers and businesses.

(5) e-CRM Utilization Technologies

① Data Warehouse: Acts as an information repository for managing various data accumulated by a company related to customers, products, and services in an integrated manner.

② Data Mining Tools: Support the analysis of accumulated data for customer support activities or direct use in marketing to enhance customer support efforts.

③ FAQ: Provides answers on the website to common questions that customers might have, helping to resolve their inquiries.

④ Call Center: A solution that responds to customer demands via phone and fax. It also supports orders and services through the web or phone.

⑤ Chatting: Implements internet chat-like formats in customer service, analyzing these interactions to effectively respond to customer demands.

⑥ Online Marketing: Supports the planning and execution of marketing activities across both online and offline channels based on data analysis.

⑦ Campaign Management: Plans and supports various campaigns tailored to the customer, and assists in analyzing campaign effectiveness using formats such as OLAP (Online Analytical Processing).

(6) Comparison of CRM and e-CRM

Category	CRM	e-CRM
Target for use	Offline-Centric Company	e-Business Company
Key Management	Sales Automation	Differentiation, Personalized Service
Customer Touchpoint	In-Person Visits, Direct Mail, Call Center	Single Integrated Channel through the Internet
Time and Space	Limited, Regional Constraints	24 Hours a Day, Worldwide
Components	Sales + Marketing + Service	e-Sales + e-Marketing + e-Service
Service	Simple Q&A using Telemarketing (TM)	Voice, Video, Multimedia

(7) Expected Effects of e-CRM

① Utilization of system resources assigned by separate numbers

② Creation of both intangible and tangible benefits

③ Improvement in customer service

④ Personalized services through individual customization
   (Conducting 1:1 marketing)

(8) Issues and Solutions of e-CRM

Issues		Solutions
Issues with Customer Data	Lack of data, Inaccuracy of data	• Collect data using integrated channels • Combine offline and online data
Issues with e-CRM Strategy	Lack of company strategy and disconnection from overall strategy	Clarify company strategy through ISP, BPR, and PI
Issues with e-CRM System	Inadequate system implementation	Specify the purpose of the implemented system
	Inappropriate analysis systems	Reflect data characteristics by analyzing the company's data tendencies in advance during the establishment of analysis systems

Service Differentiation

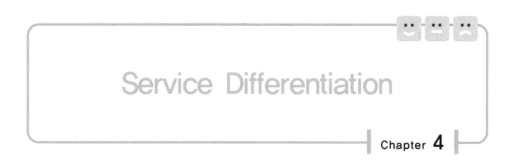

Service Differentiation

Chapter **4**

4.1 Overview of Service Differentiation

(1) Changes in Service Marketing

① The shift from a producer-centered economy to a consumer-centered economy

Rapid economic development has shifted the global economy from a producer-centered model, where products sold easily, to a consumer-centered model driven by oversupply. The incredible advancements in science and technology have made the concepts of time, distance, and location almost irrelevant, leading to globalization. As a result, a survival battle among companies has emerged worldwide, fought without traditional weapons. In this competitive environment, companies that excel in service and improve their corporate structures thrive, while those that fail to adapt are left behind.

| The Evolution of Service Marketing |

Producer-Centered Thinking   Consumer-Centered Thinking

| Changes in Service Marketing Concepts |

Production Concept	Product Concept	Selling Concept	Marketing Concept	Societal Marketing Concept

• Focus: Production and Purchase
• Assumes that consumers prefer products that are widely available and inexpensive.
• Key Points:
  1. Production-oriented market
  2. Aim to improve production efficiency and distribution coverage.
	• Focus: Product
	• Assumes that consumers favor products that offer the most quality, performance, and innovative features.
	• Key Points:
	  1. Product development and innovation
	  2. Risks of marketing myopia (focusing only on products)
		• Focus: Sales
		• Assumes that consumers will not buy enough of the firm's products unless the firm undertakes a large-scale selling and promotion effort.
		• Key Points:
		  1. Aggressive selling efforts
		  2. Customer acquisition is the priority over retention.
			• Focus: Market
			• Assumes that achieving organizational goals depends on knowing the needs and wants of target markets and delivering the desired satisfactions better than competitors.
			• Key Points:
			  1. Customer-centric approach
			  2. Integration of marketing activities
			  3. Profit through customer satisfaction
			  4. Focus on target market
			  5. Sustainable profit
				• Focus: Society's Welfare
				• Assumes that a company's marketing decisions should consider consumers' wants, the company's requirements, consumers' long-run interests, and society's long-run interests.
				• Key Points:
				  1. Green products and sustainable marketing
				  2. Social responsibility in marketing decisions

(2) Niche market

① Definition

A niche market involves targeting specific segments within a highly competitive industry, an overlooked market, or a market that is recognized but not yet fully exploited. This process includes segmenting the market and focusing on these particular niches. Niche markets are also defined formally as strategies that create smaller market segments, offering businesses protection against competition and new areas of growth[10].

② Market transformation

In the early stages, the market was characterized by mass marketing. During the 1980s, this shifted towards segmented marketing, which then evolved into niche marketing. Eventually, niche marketing transitioned into database marketing

③ Segmented marketing

Segmented marketing involves breaking down a market into smaller segments and creating specific strategies for each one. This approach categorizes the market based on criteria such as age, gender, lifestyle, and personal preferences, allowing for the development of marketing strategies tailored to the needs of each segment. For example, when a bank uses different marketing techniques for high-value clients compared to regular customers, it is employing segmented marketing.

④ Niche Marketing

After a new product is launched, its demand eventually reaches a saturation point. When this happens, companies must make strategic decisions, such as developing new products or entering new markets. However, entering an already established market late can be risky. Therefore, companies should look for markets that have not been explored or were previously considered low priority due to expected low returns on marketing investment.

---

10) Dalgic, T., & Leeuw, M. (1994). Niche Marketing Revisited: Concept, Applications and Some European Cases. European Journal of Marketing, 28, 39-55.

Broad target market   Narrow target market

A great example of market development is the creation of the 'toddler' category within children's clothing. This category targets children who are in the intermediate stage between infants and older children, specifically those who are just learning to walk. This is a case of developing a niche market by identifying and catering to a new customer segment that previously didn't exist.

Known as niche marketing, it targets markets that are overlooked or untouched by others, capitalizing on these opportunities for profit. Unlike mass marketing, niche marketing arose as customer groups became more segmented due to diverse lifestyles such as single households, DINKs (Dual Income, No Kids), and dual-income couples. This shift compelled companies to alter their traditional marketing strategies. The term "niche market" refers to the strategy of entering specific, smaller consumer groups after the decline of the mass market. However, niche marketing should not be confined to small markets alone, it can apply to both small and large markets. Regardless of size, niche marketing starts by identifying valuable, untapped segments with minimal competition.

So, what defines a good niche market? Firstly, it is a market expected to grow in the future. In such cases, the objective of niche marketing is to establish an early presence in the market. For example, beverages with green tea extracts were initially designed for health-conscious women rather than all women, but they later expanded into a large market due to the well-being trend. The watch company 'Timex' moved away from mass marketing inexpensive, long-lasting watches up until the early 1980s. Instead, they introduced limited-edition products for teenagers, differentiated products specifically for men and women, and various product lines targeting niche groups like skiers and cycling enthusiasts, which led to substantial profits.

The second trait of a good niche market is one that might not experience significant growth but is free from competitors. For instance, when three-quarter and ankle-length pants became trendy in women's fashion, anklets and toe rings became popular as ankle exposure became more common. Similarly, think of the rise of nail salons, which evolved from basic skincare to detailed hand care, or products like cellphone charms, screen protectors, and cases.

A professional who specializes in identifying good niche markets is called a niche marketer. These individuals must depart from traditional mass marketing mindsets, habits, and behaviors, and instead operate swiftly and efficiently. This approach involves making a company's activities more market and customer-centric, enabling them to adapt to rapidly changing market conditions and analyze the abundance of information to satisfy market demands. Continuous collection of various small details is essential for generating valuable ideas. As such, niche marketers must incorporate regular interaction with customers and information gathering into their daily routines.

(5) Examples of niche market (Southwest Airlines)

While most airlines competed against industry leaders like American Airlines, United Airlines, and Delta Airlines, Southwest Airlines redefined its competitive landscape by targeting a different market segment: high-speed buses and rail companies. They focused on capturing the market dominated by these transportation modes, offering a lower-cost alternative for domestic short-haul flights. This strategy appealed to travelers who found traditional airfare too expensive and were willing to endure longer travel times by car or train.

Southwest Airlines concentrated on this niche by providing affordable short-distance flights, effectively attracting passengers who previously thought air travel was out of reach and those who typically drove. As a result, the short-haul travel market created by Southwest Airlines experienced higher growth rates compared to the overall airline market. By appealing to people who viewed airfare as too costly and those who relied on cars for travel, Southwest successfully pioneered a new market segment.

| Examples of Niche Marketing |

Tesla - Enviornmentally concious

Häagen-Dazs - Icecream for adults

Whole Foods Market - Health concious

Aesop - Premium skincare product

⑥ Database marketing

Database marketing refers to the collection and analysis of various customer-related data to maximize marketing efficiency. It evolves into individual marketing, one-to-one marketing, and relationship marketing, all of which focus on maintaining unique, personalized, and ongoing relationships with customers.

⑦ Niche Market and the Long Tail Principle

The Long Tail principle suggests that in online stores with a vast array of products, the majority of sales come from niche items that usually have low sales volumes and are challenging to stock in physical stores. This idea contrasts with the Pareto principle in offline stores, where 20% of top-selling items account for 80% of total sales. In online stores, when you plot the sales curve for each product, the sales of niche items form a long, thin tail, similar to an animal's tail, hence the name.

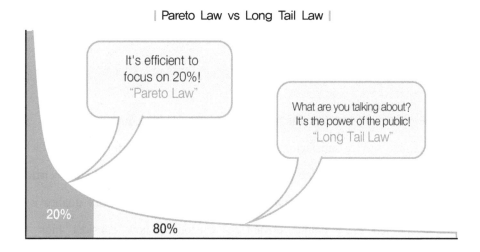

| Pareto Law vs Long Tail Law |

⑧ The Formation of Niche Markets and Customer-Centric Organizational Culture

Niche markets can be created by understanding customers through continuous and effective communication. To facilitate this, it is crucial to develop an organizational culture where customers feel comfortable reaching out to the company and sharing even the smallest details.

4.2   Service Paradox

(1) Overview of Service Paradox

① Definition

The term "Service Paradox" refers to the phenomenon whereby, despite greater economic prosperity and access to a wider range of services than before, satisfaction with those services is declining.

② Two Determining Factors of the Service Paradox: High Expectations and Actual Service Performance

The causes of the service paradox can be divided into two factors that determine service satisfaction: expectations of service performance and actual service performance. One primary cause is the rise in customer expectations. For instance, in the telecommunications industry, superior call quality is no longer seen as a unique advantage. Customers now consider high call quality to be a fundamental feature of any telecom service. If companies cannot meet these elevated expectations with innovative service offerings, customer satisfaction will inevitably decrease.

(2) Causes and Solutions of the Service Paradox

To understand the phenomenon of the service paradox, we must explore the industrialization of services, where marketing theories from the manufacturing sector are directly applied to the service industry.

Service industrialization involves replacing labor-intensive aspects of service activities with machinery to improve efficiency and cut costs. It also means applying planning, organization, training, control, and management techniques used in automobile production to service activities.

Although service industrialization has led to increased efficiency in many areas, it also presents several limitations.

① Standardization of Services

The lack of employee discretion and the essential human element of service leads to a perception of service poverty amid a prosperous service economy.

② Homogenization of Services

There is a risk of offering standardized services in areas that require differentiation, leading to rigidity and an inability to adapt to various situations. In the pursuit of maintaining service uniformity, the crucial element of individuality in services is lost.

③ Loss of Humanity in Services

In the process of industrializing service companies, focusing solely on efficiency can lead to treating employees as mere cogs in a machine, echoing the dehumanization seen during the evolution of manufacturing industries. As labor costs rise and the number of employees remains limited amidst skyrocketing service demands, employees can become mentally and physically exhausted. This often results in them behaving mechanically when interacting with numerous customers. In the service industry, such declines in employee morale and mental fatigue directly impact service quality, making the loss of humanity a more severe issue compared to manufacturing.

④ Technology Complexity

Products have become so complex that consumers and employees sometimes struggle to keep up with technological advancements. The era of easily getting repairs at a nearby shop is over; now, customers often have to travel farther and wait longer for service.

⑤ The Vicious Cycle of Employee Recruitment

As recruiting personnel becomes more challenging, companies often hire employees without sufficient training, leading to the design of tasks that require minimal skills. This situation lowers employee morale and leaves them unprepared to handle problems effectively. Consequently, wages are reduced, and jobs become simplified. Additionally, when employees are promoted or leave, customers end up being served by inexperienced staff, which inevitably results in a decline in service quality.

(3) Strategies to Overcome the Service Paradox

S (sincerity, speed & smile)	: Service should encompass sincerity, speed, and a smile.
E (energy)	: Service should be full of vibrant energy.
R (revolutionary)	: Service should be fresh and innovative.
V (valuable)	: Service should be valuable.
I (impressive)	: Service should be impressive.
C (communication)	: Service should include communication.
E (entertainment)	: Service should be about welcoming customers.

4.3 · Service Failure

(1) Definition of Service Failure

According to various scholars, service failure is defined as "Where customer dissatisfaction arises during interactions with the customer". This can occur in interactions between the company and the customer or between the service provider and the customer. Susan Keaveney emphasized that service failure is a crucial factor in customer defection or switching behavior in service contexts. She identified the failure to deliver core value as the primary cause, followed by unfriendly customer service, and discussed the types and impacts of customer defection from companies.

(2) The Importance of Service Failure

The importance of service failure lies in its impact on future transactions between customers and the company, as well as on attracting new customers through word-of-mouth. A single negative experience can create a halo effect, affecting the overall perception of the company. Additionally, a service failure in one area can trigger failures in other areas, leading to a domino effect. Therefore, addressing service failures is critically important.

(3) Service Recovery Definition

Grönroos (1988)[11] posited that service failures due to negative mismatch lead to customer dissatisfaction, but effective service recovery can restore customer satisfaction. If a company fails to recover from a service issue, it can further

---

11) Gronroos, C. (1988). Service Quality: The Six Criteria of Good Perceived Service Quality. Review of Business, 9, 10-13.

disappoint already dissatisfied customers. On the other hand, successful service recovery can turn dissatisfied customers into loyal ones who are more likely to return. Care must be taken during the recovery process to avoid the double-deviation effect, which can exacerbate dissatisfaction. Research indicates that most customer complaints stem not only from service failures but also from the attitudes of employees handling these issues. Service recovery can be divided into two main types: psychological recovery (involving apologies and empathy) and tangible recovery (involving compensation for financial losses and inconveniences).

(4) Service Recovery Paradox Definition

The service recovery paradox is a theory suggesting that effectively addressing a service failure can lead to higher customer satisfaction than if the failure had never occurred. This means that customer satisfaction can actually be greater after a successful service recovery than it was before the failure. Abrams and Paese noted that proactive efforts to resolve service failures can create a strong bond with customers, resulting in higher engagement and increased likelihood of repurchase.

(5) Factors Influencing the Service Recovery Paradox

① Equity Theory

According to Adams' equity theory[12], individuals feel a sense of injustice when they believe their outcomes are inferior compared to others. This sense of fairness is assessed by comparing the effort and resources they invest with the results they receive. Steve Brown and Steve Lex identified

---

12) Adams, J. S. (1963). Towards an understanding of inequity. The Journal of Abnormal and Social Psychology, 67(5), 422-436.

three types of fairness that customers expect in service failure resolution: outcome fairness, procedural fairness, and interactional fairness.

Outcome fairness involves receiving compensation that matches the level of dissatisfaction, such as future free services, monetary compensation, repairs and exchanges, or discounts. Procedural fairness pertains to the methods used to handle the service failure, including company policies, procedures, and timeliness. Interactional fairness focuses on the behavior of service employees, with customers expecting respectful, considerate, and friendly treatment.

② Attribution Theory

Attribution theory involves understanding the causes and significance of an event when it occurs. For customers, this means perceiving the reasons behind what they observe and experience. They identify the cause of the current situation, make inferences about it, and then decide on their final attitude or behavior towards the subject based on these inferences.

Attribution Theory
a theory of the process of inferring the cause of an action
- Internal attribution: finding the cause of the action in the person's personality or temperament
- External attribution: finding the cause of action in perjury situations or environmental factors

What a nice kid~

Are you trying to l ook good to infront of your girlfriend?

Internal attribution

External attribution

(6) Service Recovery Expectations

Customer satisfaction is achieved when the service provided aligns with their expectations. People typically evaluate services based on their beliefs and past experiences. In the event of a service failure, customers expect to understand the cause and for the company to take responsibility. Research shows that customer dissatisfaction can reach 86% when a company fails to respond to a service failure. However, if the company issues a proper apology and addresses the issue, dissatisfaction drops to 20%.

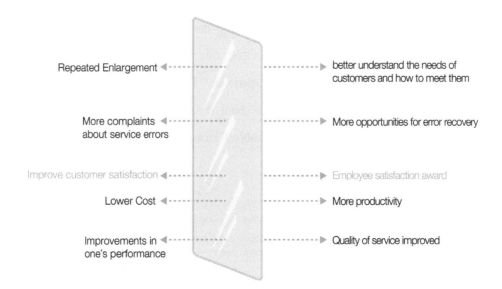

Repeated Enlargement ◄ ········· ········· ► better understand the needs of customers and how to meet them

More complaints about service errors ◄ ········· ········· ► More opportunities for error recovery

Improve customer satisfaction ◄ ········· ········· ► Employee satisfaction award

Lower Cost ◄ ········· ········· ► More productivity

Improvements in one's performance ◄ ········· ········· ► Quality of service improved

4.4 ⟿ Points of Service

(1) Overview

A service master must clearly understand the key service points and provide the service accordingly to achieve customer delight.

(2) 7 Key Service Points

① Product

    a. Service is the ultimate product.

    b. Service determines the quality of the product.

    c. Design the service before the functionality, performance, and lifespan of the product.

② Customer

    a. Customers should not just be seen as sales targets but as individuals to be impressed and delighted.

    b. Customers are more than just buyers of products; they are individuals who should be satisfied and have their quality of life enhanced.

    c. Not every consumer in the market is my customer; only those who find satisfaction in the service are true customers.

③ Future

    a. Invisible services determine the future of the company.

    b. Service, though intangible and unseen, carries immense potential.

④ Purchase

    a. Customers do not pay for products; they invest in satisfaction.

    b. Unsatisfied customers do not make repeat purchases.

    c. Customer satisfaction becomes a factor in their investment.

⑤ Impressing Customer

    a. The key to excellent service lies in promptly implementing what is commonly perceived as necessary.

    b. It's not about creating something groundbreaking or inventing entirely new methods. It's about consistently delivering timely and expected

⑥ Facial Expression

    a. Don't come to work if you're not going to smile.

    b. A smile is equivalent to service.

    c. Warm service doesn't start from the mind but from a warm smile.

    d. A smile is the best and most perfect uniform.

    e. Fancy interiors, spacious stores, and delicious food are all in vain if the staff lose their smiles.

⑦ Professionalism

    a. The power to satisfy customers is only possible when employees themselves are satisfied.

    b. Employees are primarily the ones who need to be satisfied.

    c. Employee satisfaction is the key to improving the quality of service.

4.5 ⊷ The Importance of A/S (After Sales)

(1) Overview

"After Service (A/S)" refers to the ongoing services provided by a seller after a product has been sold. These services include repairs, installation, inspections, and other forms of support. For instance, this encompasses offering repair services either free of charge or at a discounted rate, maintaining a ready stock of spare parts, and ensuring quality assurance for extended periods. Such commitments foster trust in the store or product, cultivating a loyal customer base over time.

(2) Importance

When customers decide to purchase a product, they consider not just the product itself but also the after-sales service. This makes a significant difference between salespeople who actively manage customer relationships through A/S and those who do not. For instance, by consistently providing thorough A/S and ensuring customer satisfaction, salespeople can receive referrals from happy customers, leading to rapid growth where each referral could potentially bring in around 30 new customers through a five-stage process. This naturally creates a pyramid or multi-level sales structure. Conversely, neglecting A/S may result in losing over 30 potential customers. Therefore, A/S is just as crucial as the sales process itself.

(3) Key Principles of A/S

① Step 1 (Providing according to customer demands)

By confidently providing products or services that precisely meet customer demands, we reassure customers. For example, if we install an air conditioner, demonstrating its operation on-site to verify its performance aligns with this approach.

② Step 2 (Verification of satisfaction)

To verify the satisfaction of the product or service, we make phone calls or visits. For example, even after 2-3 days, we may visit or call to ask, "Is the air conditioner working well?" or "Are there any issues you are experiencing?" These messages aim to ensure that customers who have purchased the air conditioner are pleased and satisfied.

③ Step 3 (Handling complaints)

In the course of using the product, customers will be able to address failures or complaints quickly and effectively

④ Step 4 (maintain intimacy and search for information)

a. In the following step, regardless of whether there is special business to be conducted, visit under the pretense of investigating the status of use and stay in close contact with the customer.

b. The natural tendency of these individuals is to collect information about the people around them, and, if possible, they are introduced directly to the individual they may be interested in purchasing from.

⑤ Step 5 (providing information and building trust)

Through the provision of information on additional products and services that may be available from time to time, the company builds trust.

A Case Study on
Service Differentiation

A Case Study on
Service Differentiation

A Case Study on Service Differentiation

Chapter **5**

5.1 Service Differentiation Factors

A service differentiation strategy consists of planning and implementing a special awareness of service products at the physical, human, and systemic levels.

(1) Physical Services Differentiation

Intangible services are categorized by physical elements, such as buildings, facilities, interiors, and food. When most customers are willing to pay high prices, the physical service must be differentiated. When visiting a hotel, you would expect to receive a much higher level of physical service compared to an inn even if the price is higher.

(2) Human Services Differentiation

Customers who are willing to pay high prices expect the human services to be differentiated. The human service at a hotel's high-end restaurant is likely to be differentiated from the human service at a fast food restaurant, for example.

(3) Systemic service differentiation

A system of service differentiation, such as the means and routes of communication, plays an important role in forming a customer's perception of service levels. This means that the level of service can be measured by the level of corporate image integration (CI: Corporate Identity), advertising, and the presence of Internet information services and their content, as well as design. For example, assuming there are two service companies with the same level of physical service and human service processes, we can identify the companies which have well-developed CI, are engaged in advertising, and are able to differentiate those that provide systematic services, such as Internet information services, from those that do not provide such services.

5.2 ⋅⋅ Customer Recognition Program

(1) Customer Recognition Value

The concept of value can be described as an abstract belief and it represents an individual's belief in an ideal state of being or an ideal pattern of behavior. It is believed that the concept of value varies depending on a customer's priority situation and background, and how a customer perceives value is also different based on an individual's perspective. Human behavior can be influenced by values in a number of ways, and values also demonstrate the rationale behind individual behavior. It refers to a mental expression of an important end state to be reached in one's life, and can be subjective, intangible, or symbolic.

(2) Cognitive Factors

Cognitive knowledge refers to an individual's beliefs, attitudes, behaviors, and environment. There are different types of relationships, first of all it is important to note that there is no relationship between the elements in a person's cognitive structure that involves one cognition not being obliged to another cognition. Furthermore there are two more different types which are, harmonious relationships between cognitions that are unified or coincident, and mismatched relationships between cognitions that conflict. Inconsistencies in cognitive elements can lead to conflicts in behavior or attitude when they arise. Therefore, most individuals hope that their beliefs, attitudes, language, and behavior are consistent. Instead of adjusting their beliefs according to their behavior, consumers adjust their beliefs according to their behavior.

(3) Cognitive Dissonance

The theory of cognitive dissonance put forward by Festinger[13] suggests that consumers' perceptions of what is right and what is wrong are psychological states when the perceptions are in conflict. During times of dissonance, harmony must be achieved between elements that lack balance so that psychological anxiety or tension may be reduced. An individual who has recently purchased an expensive automobile will pay more attention to product advertisements than an individual who has never purchased such a vehicle. As a result, I want to believe that the behavior of purchasing an expensive vehicle was appropriate. It is a form of 'cognitive coordination' in which one tries to 'feel good' by enjoying one's new automobile.

---

13) Festinger, L. (1957). A theory of cognitive dissonance. Stanford University Press.

(4) Ritz—Carlton Hotel Customer's Recognition Program

① Overview

The Ritz-Carlton Hotel is renowned for offering differentiated, individualized services rather than standardized, uniform services to all customers. The key to enabling such highly personalized services is the hotel's customer information management system, known as the 'Customer Recognition Program'. This system ensures that even if a customer has visited the Ritz-Carlton only once, the hotel can access stored information in the database about the customer's preferences, interests, and likes. This allows the hotel to provide services tailored to the customer's tastes, regardless of which location worldwide they stay at.

② Customer Coordinator

Each Ritz-Carlton Hotel chain has one or two customer coordinators whose main responsibilities are to research individual customer preferences and provide differentiated services for each customer. When a list of reserved customers is obtained, the customer coordinator accesses the customer history database, which stores information about interactions between the customer and any Ritz-Carlton Hotel chain location, to understand the customer's personal preferences.

③ Maximization of Customer Satisfaction

The Ritz-Carlton Hotel utilizes the Customer Recognition Program to provide services that anticipate and fulfill customer desires without them having to express their needs. By using customer information to offer sincere and dedicated service, the Ritz-Carlton Hotel maximizes customer satisfaction.

(5) The Ritz-Carlton Hotel's Golden Standards

① The Credo

   a. Our most important mission is to provide our customers with a truly comfortable and cozy environment.

   b. We pledge to offer each and every customer the highest quality of service and facilities so that they can always enjoy a warm and luxurious atmosphere.

   c. The experience at the Ritz-Carlton Hotel will invigorate our customers' lives, make them realize true well-being, and fulfill their hidden desires and hopes.

② The Motto

"We are Ladies and Gentlemen Serving Ladies and Gentlemen"

③ 3 Levels of Service

   a. Warm and sincere greeting, addressing the customer by name whenevers possible

   b. Anticipate and meet the customer's needs before they express them.

   c. Express gratitude with a warm farewell, using the customer's name whenever possible, and bid them a warm farewell.

5.3 · Service Profit Chain

(1) Overview

One of the prominent concepts in recent service management discussions is the "Service Profit Chain". Developed by Heskett, Sasser, and Schlesinger[14] of Harvard University, profitability is primarily driven by market share is not precise, asserting instead that revenue growth and profitability are influenced by customer loyalty. They argue that highly satisfied employees lead to higher customer loyalty and productivity, which in turn attract loyal customers.

(2) Definition

The service profit chain refers to the logical structure where customer service becomes the source of revenue. In other words, it represents a series of relationships connecting profitability, customer loyalty, employee satisfaction, employee retention, and productivity. The increase in a company's profitability stems from customer loyalty, which is influenced by the satisfaction resulting from the perceived value of the services provided. The value of service is created by employees who are satisfied with their jobs and demonstrate high productivity. If internal customers, the employees, are not satisfied, high-value services cannot be delivered.

(3) The Structure of the Service Profit Chain

① Internal Structure

    a. Internal service quality leads to employee satisfaction.

---

14) Heskett, J. L., Sasser, W. E., & Schlesinger, L. A. (2010). The value profit chain: Treat employees like customers and customers like. Simon and Schuster.

b. Employee satisfaction leads to employee loyalty.

c. Employee loyalty leads to employee productivity.

② Service Value

Employee productivity leads to the creation of service value.

③ External Structure

a. Service value leads to customer satisfaction.

b. Customer satisfaction increases customer loyalty.

c. Revenue and growth are connected to customer loyalty. If customer loyalty increases by 5%, revenue typically increases by 25% to 85%.

(4) Satisfaction Mirror

The term "Satisfaction Mirror" was used in a paper by Benjamin Schneider and David Bowen[15]. In their 1985 report based on studies conducted in banks, insurance companies, hospitals, and other settings, they highlighted a close relationship between customer and employee satisfaction levels. They found that if frontline employees who interact with customers have poor service levels, it leads to decreased customer satisfaction and naturally reduces revenue for the company. Conversely, when employees find meaning in their work, exert effort, and feel satisfied, they provide better service that naturally increases customer satisfaction and leads to increased revenue. This concept is known as the satisfaction mirror theory.

---

15) Schneider, B., & Bowen, D. E. (1985). Employee and customer perceptions of service in banks: Replication and extension. Journal of Applied Psychology, 70(3), 423‒433.

5.4 Customer-centric Product Differentiation

(1) The Significance of Product Differentiation Strategy

By emphasizing characteristics that distinguish them from competing products, differentiation strategy aims to secure a competitive advantage. Successful differentiation allows companies to potentially monopolize specific segments of the market, giving them the power to command higher prices from consumers. In situations where technological product quality levels are similar, modern consumers' diverse needs increasingly value even small differences between products. Consequently, the importance of customer-centric product differentiation strategies is growing.

(2) Types of Product Differentiation Strategies

① Customer Segmentation Strategy

Customer segmentation is the process of dividing customers into groups with similar needs and developing marketing strategies for each group. In the past, segmentation was primarily based on demographic factors such as gender, age, location, and income. However, nowadays, to tailor products and services to individual customers effectively, segmentation needs to consider more nuanced factors such as preferences, personality, lifestyle, and behavior.

② Diversification of Model Customers

In the complex landscape of consumer segmentation, the most effective strategy for businesses is diversification of model customers. In the future, consumers will not exist as large homogeneous groups. They will be scattered like points, transcending simple demographic criteria and centered around various variables. Therefore, businesses need to identify consumers who play central roles at multiple points and focus on their psychology and behaviors. By doing so, they can efficiently grasp the evolving diversity and individualization of consumers, allowing them to develop appropriate responses tailored to each customer's needs.

③ Adjusting to Extreme Market Changes

The trend towards personalization in society has brought about polarization in consumer behavior as well. In the future, consumers will exhibit price-sensitive consumption patterns for basic necessities with low emotional involvement. Conversely, they will be willing to pay high prices for products they consider personally important, such as those that reflect their values or social status. The challenge lies in adapting to this differentiation trend; companies that target the "General Public" without adapting may struggle to survive. The low-cost market will favor distribution companies with strong global sourcing capabilities, while the high-end market will be dominated by companies with strong positioning and brand power. Therefore, clearly defining and differentiating strategies tailored to their target markets will be essential for survival in this competitive landscape. Recent market research underscores these trends, as seen in the U.S. vodka market where high-end Ketel One and low-end McCormick are gaining market share, while mid-range Smirnoff struggles to exceed single-digit market share.

④ Expansion of Mass Customization Adaptation

Alvin Toffler foresaw in his 1970[16] book "Future Shock" that the era of cost reduction through production efficiency and profit from economies of scale has passed. The shift in market perception was systematized by Stan Davis in his book "Future Perfect", where he coined the term "Mass Customization". Mass Customization combines mass production with customization, enabling the fulfillment of diverse demands and expectations of individual customers while maintaining low costs through mass production. This became feasible with the dramatic advancements in information and production technologies.

In the era of standardized mass production, ordinary customers were willing to give up their preferences and accept standardized products at an adequate level, not just the affluent. However, uniqueness among individual customers did not disappear entirely. Customers still desired products tailored to their specific needs, each harboring a variety of requirements. Now, acknowledging that within each individual customer there exist multiple needs that can constitute a market for businesses, companies must recognize and find the most suitable ways to approach personalized customers. This recognition underscores why Mass Customization has become crucially important and why, without this concept, businesses risk becoming obsolete in the global market.

---

16) Toffler, A. (2021). Future shock. Random House.

5.5 ⊶ Future-oriented Services

(1) Overview

The airline transportation industry is one of the rapidly growing sectors within the global economy, keeping pace with the trend of globalization. However, today's global circumstances have led the aviation industry into an unprecedented downturn due to political and social instability such as wars, aircraft terrorism, epidemics, and economic instability like fluctuating exchange rates and oil prices. In these challenging realities, many airlines are facing the threat of bankruptcy, with numerous airlines worldwide having already declared bankruptcy.

In times as difficult as these, airlines must attract customers through the development of competitive advantage products and efforts of their own. The impact is profound domestically with a sharp decline in domestic air passengers due to low-cost carriers and internationally with the competition faced by many foreign airlines.

In the middle of these challenging times in the aviation industry, let's examine Singapore Airlines as a case study that has pioneered forward-looking services.

(2) Singapore Airport Case

Singapore Airlines unveiled its latest generation of airline services, led by four years of research and development with an investment of $360 million USD. Meticulously designed to offer Singapore Airlines' exceptional service, the First Class, Business Class, and Economy Class cabins are crafted with premium quality and style. The First and Business Class seats, which convert into fully flat beds, not only represent the largest in the airline industry but also provide significantly expanded personal space compared to previous offerings. KrisWorld, Singapore Airlines' in-flight entertainment system, is poised to establish a new concept in in-flight services with over a thousand entertainment programs and office software capabilities. Customers of Singapore Airlines played a pivotal role in this airline service development, contributing feedback and advice from the initial introduction of the in-flight service project through design reviews and testing phases. A Singapore Airlines spokesperson noted, "Through customer feedback and advice, we were able to understand what customers want in airline services". They further emphasized, "Customer insights have provided a clear diagnosis of what the future in-flight experience with Singapore Airlines should be".

5.6　Customized Patient Services in Hospitals

(1) Characteristics of Medical Services

Medical services have distinct characteristics among service industries. I would like to outline the characteristics of medical services into three points.

① Most Services take Place in front of the Customer's Eyes.

When we go to a service center to repair home appliances or cell phones, we submit the faulty item and wait in the waiting room. The visible area where this happens is called the Front Office. Beyond the counter, the actual repair of the product takes place, and the space behind it, which we cannot see, is called the Back Office. In a department store, the store itself is the Front Office, and the warehouse is the Back Office. In a restaurant, the tables where guests eat are in the Front Office, and the kitchen is the

Back Office. The Front Office primarily serves customers, while the Back Office handles tasks such as food preparation in restaurants or repairing faulty items.

However, what about hospitals? Procedures must be conducted in front of the patient. There is almost no distinction between Front and Back in hospitals. It's difficult to say that even the operating room is the Back Office if surgeries are performed under local anesthesia without general anesthesia. There is hardly anywhere to hide from the patient's view in hospitals. Medical practitioners such as doctors and nurses must constantly interact with customers, meaning how staff treat customers decisively affects customer satisfaction.

② The Treatment Process Itself Affects the Outcomes Perceived by the Patient.

A patient went for an endoscopy. When the nurse called them in, she accidentally called out someone else's name. Before the endoscopy, during the consultation with the doctor, the attending physician spent a long time on the phone, appearing to get angry with someone. After the endoscopy, the patient feels uneasy. There is a suspicion that the doctor may have made a mistake during the procedure. In reality, the discomfort after the endoscopy could be unrelated to the nurse's mistake in calling out the name or the doctor's phone call during the consultation. However, the patient doesn't think so. Pain is subjective, so the patient's perception of the care received during the treatment process affects the outcome. Therefore, how patients are treated and the attitude with which they are approached during treatment can influence the effectiveness of their care.

③ Every Patient is Unique.

The disease state of patients varies with each patient. Each patient has different nutritional statuses, different types of bacteria causing infections, and their intestines are positioned differently. To use a manufacturing industry, it's like the composition of materials used varies each time. Despite using different materials, the same results are expected, which requires the experience and expertise of medical professionals. Moreover, not only do patients differ in their physical conditions, but also in their personalities and tolerance levels of pain. Some may scream as if they are dying from a simple injection needle, while others endure the pain of bone scraping. Furthermore, patients have diverse personalities, some might brush off minor side effects assuming they will disappear on their own without even calling the treating doctor, whereas others insist they are wrong even when there is no evidence of an issue and demand compensation. Therefore, both medical treatment skills and customer service skills as a healthcare provider are equally crucial.

(2) Changes in the Medical Service Environment

① Changes in Business Environment

As a result of recent changes in the medical environment, the bankruptcy problem of small and medium-sized hospitals has reached a serious level, and the bankruptcy rate of hospitals after the division of medicine is more than 15 times higher than that of general companies. Furthermore, the medical management environment is experiencing rapid changes due to an increase in the number of physicians, an increase in wages, the introduction of comprehensive fee systems, the introduction of fee contracts, the establishment of medical review and evaluation agencies, and the introduction of elective treatment systems.

② Changes in the Medical Environment

As living standards have improved and living environments have changed, so has the composition of diseases. Chronic degenerative diseases, accidents, and pollution diseases are on the rise, and the demand for health promotion services is also on the rise as a result of changes in the concept of health. Additionally, due to the rapid progression of the aging process, there is an increasing demand for senile diseases and chronic diseases. In contrast, the demand for medical services related to obstetrics and gynecology and pediatrics continues to decrease as a result of improved health levels due to increased income and the decrease in fertility rates as a result of women's entry into society. The number of people visiting beauty-related hospitals is increasing as a result of women's entry into society, in order to express their beauty and favor others.

③ An Appropriate Direction of Change

In today's rapidly changing medical environment, hospitals should not only provide basic treatment functions, but also provide treatment that values humans and takes into account the natural environment. Moreover, the hospital should be a forward-looking facility so as to be able to respond to future growth and change while improving the quality of care for individual patients.

a. The hospital serves as a service institution as well.

b. It is necessary to break away from authoritarian practices and create a hospital that customers will want to return to.

c. In the patient's perspective, the hospital interior is designed.

d. Engage customer management experts.

Service Marketing

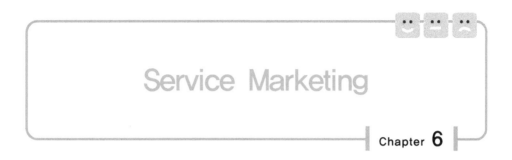

Service Marketing

Chapter **6**

6.1 Customer Segmentation – STP Analysis

(1) Market Segmentation

① Definition of Market Segmentation

Market segmentation is the process of dividing the entire market into smaller segments with similar needs, based on the idea that one product cannot meet all unique consumer needs simultaneously. Essentially, it is the process of dividing the entire market into homogenous groups with similar needs or significant sales activities in order to develop a more effective marketing mix.

Additional Information **STP(Segmentation Targeting Positioning) Strategy**

It refers to a marketing strategy that divides the entire market by consumer groups with similar needs, selects or targets the most suitable segmented market for the company by evaluating the attractiveness of each segmented market, and positions the most desirable competitive position in the selected target market.

② Market Segmentation Criteria

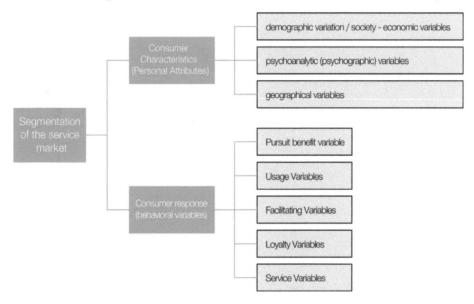

a. Demographic and socioeconomic variables

- Demographic variables: gender, age, size of family, family life cycle, etc
- Social statistical variables: income, education level, social class, etc

b. Psychoanalytic (psycho—ecological, psycho—graphic) variables

Among the various personal characteristics of consumers, market segmentation is different according to a person's behavior, personality, or way of life

example) Lifestyle, social class, personality, etc

c. Geographic variable: It is one of the criteria for segmentation frequently considered by service companies because of its low cost and relatively easy method.

example) the area of residence, the size of the city (number of people), climate, population density, etc

d. Behavioral variables

- Pursuit Benefits (Pursuit of Benefits): How to segment markets under the assumption that the benefits that consumers seek may differ fundamentally for a single service

  example) The clothing market is segmented into a group of consumers seeking identity symbolism, fashionability, practicality, and economic feasibility according to the benefits consumers seek when purchasing clothing products

- Usage Variables : Most service markets can be divided into large users, heavy users, small users, or non-user groups, and can be segmented according to the degree or type of service use.

- Facilitating Response Variables : The market is segmented based on the consumer's response to the company's specific promotion activities, where response refers to the consumer's response to the service company's advertising, sales promotion, display or exhibition.

  example) Consumer analysis based on service preference usage method, etc.

- Loyalty Variables : Loyalty is the degree of consistency in which consumers steadily purchase specific products or services, which is the psychology of consumers who love and prefer specific trademarks, that is, consumers' preference to prefer specific trademarks according to the purpose of use and purchase them repeatedly.

  example) Divide into stubborn loyalists, decent loyalists, variable loyalists, and converter

- Service Variables : It is important to recognize that one of the areas that has received relatively little attention in market segmentation is the type of customer response to various service providers. Several factors contribute to the quality of customer service, including the differentiation at the level of service. It is possible to design a suitable package of services for an individual segmented market based on these factors.

Additional
Information **Definition and Classification of Markets**

A market is a place where an exchange between a buyer and a seller takes place, and is defined as "a set of current and potential customers who have a specific need and are willing to engage in an exchange to satisfy that need".

- **Consumer market** : Customers in this market buy products or services for their final consumption.

- **Industrial market** : Customers in this market purchase specific products or services to produce other products or services

- **Government market** : It consists of the central government and local governments, and mainly purchases products and services for service and defense to the people.

- **Reseller market** : It consists of distributors who purchase a product or service and sell it to other markets, such as wholesalers and retailers.

- **Institutional market** : This market consists of churches, private schools, hospitals, and charities that buy products and services only for end-use, not for personal profit.

- **International market** : It consists of customers in different countries, which may include all five markets described above.

(2) Target Market Selection

Target markets are subdivided markets in which a service provider develops and applies its marketing mix.

① Requirements for Target Market

    a. Measurability: that a marketing manager should be able to measure the size or purchasing power of each segment of the market.

    b. Maintenance: that a segmented market should be large enough in terms of size and revenue.

    c. Accessibility: that effective marketing efforts should enable them to reach segmental markets and serve them by appropriate means.

    d. Viability: Whether a service company has the ability to plan and execute effective marketing programs sufficiently to meet the needs of customers in each segment of the market

② How to Select a Target Market

    a. A Non-differentiation Strategy (Mass Marketing)

      • As a result of this strategy, the market is viewed as a homogenous group rather than a collection of heterogeneous needs, and a single marketing mix program is intended to target the largest segment of the market.

      • It is possible to achieve economies of scale in marketing and production. In other words, because the cost of market research and segmentation is reduced, and only one service is provided, R&D and management costs are saved (a single service), inventory costs, transportation costs, and advertising costs can be reduced through mass distribution and mass advertising, thereby reducing promotional costs.

      • The disadvantage is that if several companies use the same strategy in the same segmented market, fierce competition occurs, and as a result, large segmented markets show severe competition, making it more difficult to earn profits and less likely to succeed.

| Non-differentiation Strategy |

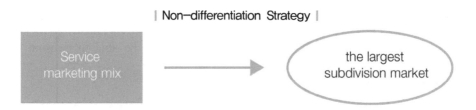

b. Differentiation Strategy

- It refers to an approach that selects two or more subdivided markets as target markets and provides unique services suitable for each subdivided market.

- Since various services are provided at various prices and in various forms to meet the needs of different consumers and sales promotion is carried out using multiple distribution channels, more consumers can be secured as customers, increasing total sales.

- It is an appropriate positioning method for large companies with abundant resources to invest in multiple segment markets at the same time because different services must be provided for each segment.

| Differentiation Strategy |

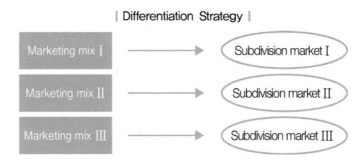

c. Centralization Strategy

• A number of small and medium-sized enterprises with limited available resources choose one or several segmented markets (gap markets) that provide them with the greatest competitive advantage instead of maintaining a low share in the large market and then secure a high share within this market.

• It has the advantage of being able to build a strong market position in a segmented market because it can precisely analyze the needs and characteristics of consumers in the target market, thereby developing the optimal marketing mix and deeply penetrating the target market, thereby increasing sales and establishing a strong market position through specialization. Additionally, it is suitable for small and medium-sized businesses that lack resources because it costs less.

• Companies must take a higher risk because the risk from market uncertainty is large.

| Centralization Strategy |

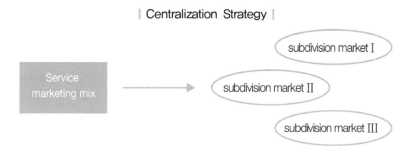

③ Marketing Strategy according to Target Market Selection Method

Category	Non-differentiation marketing strategy	Differention marketing strategy	Centralization Strategy
Market Definition	A wide range of customers	Two or more limited customer groups	Single well-defined customer group
Cost	Reduce cost	Increase cost	The highest cost increase
Product Strategy	Selling a limited number of products and services to a single brand for a wide range of customers	Provide a separate product or service that is appropriate for each customer group	Delivering a single brand of products or services to a single consumer group
Price Strategy	An overall single price	Differentiation price	A single price
Distribution Strategy	Mobilize all possible sales channels	Selection of differentiation media according to segmental market	Specialized media such as specialized social media
Promotion Strategy	Mass media	Selection of differentiation media according to segmental market	Specialized media such as specialized social media
Goal	A competitive advantage	Homogeneous needs and preferences	Acquirement of market
Importance of Strategy	Access to different types of consumers through the same marketing program	Access two or more markets with differentiated marketing strategies for each segment	Access specific consumer groups through the same highly specialized marketing program
Risk Burden	Small	Medium	Large
Way of thinking	Business-oriented thinking	Customer-focused thinking	A customer-friendly thinking

④ Market Segmentation

Uncertainty concerning the customer's needs can make it difficult for a purchase to be converted into an actual purchase. Therefore, it is necessary to set the criteria for segmenting the entire purchasing market and identify the segmented market. Market segmentation is the adjustment of marketing or products in response to the customer needs of each segmented market across a wide range of entire markets. Recently, rather than mass marketing, marketing is gradually changing to segmented markets, niche markets, and regional markets.

This market segmentation can present the advantages of being able to set sales promotion costs only for high-profit segmented markets, to set products to suit the needs of segmented markets, and to plan and prepare for future markets.

Kotler (2007) [17] presented customer segmentation requirements based on five criteria: measurability, accessibility, practicality, and actionability differentiation for effective market segmentation. As for customer segmentation methods, there are possible market segmentation methods in the consumer goods market and the industrial goods market.

a. Possible Market Segmentation Methods in Consumer Market

- Geographical standards : a country, city/rural, climate, etc

- Demographic criteria : age, gender, occupation, religion, education level, income, family size, nationality, social class, etc

- Criteria for purchasing behavior : Brand affinity, usage, frequency of use, price sensitivity, and important variables (service, quality, economy, speed, etc.)

- Psychological criteria : Attitudes, role models, lifestyles, personalities, personalities, etc

b. Possible Market Segmentation Methods in Industrial Market

- Demographic criteria : Industry size, industry type, company size, technology, location, etc

- Operational standards : Customer capability, recruitment skills, status of users and non-users, etc

---

17) Kotler, P., & Pfoertsch, W. (2007). Being known or being one of many: the need for brand management for business-to-business (B2B) companies. Journal of business & industrial marketing, 22(6), 357-362.

- Habitual criteria for purchasing : Purchase criteria, authority structure, purchasing function organization, etc
- Situational criteria : Purchase size, urgency of purchase, special purpose, etc
- Personal characteristics : loyalty, attitude toward risk, similarity between buyers and sellers

(3) Service Positioning

① The Concept of Positioning

a. It refers to taking some action in the minds of potential customers, not taking any action on a product or service. In other words, positioning is what determines the location of a product or service in the mind of potential customers - how customers perceive that product or service.

b. The position of a product or service means how consumers perceive competing products based on certain attributes.

c. Positioning can also be defined as finding, developing, and communicating competitive advantages that make customers perceive a particular organization's products or services as superior and at the same time distinguishing them from competitors' products or services in the minds of target customers.

② The Importance of Positioning

a. Ultimately, positioning refers to the proper use of it to suit the organization, service, and target market as a differentiation strategy. This differentiation can be based on subjective criteria such as images and communication, or it can be based on objective criteria such as the components of the service marketing mix such as products, processes, human resources, and customer service.

b. It can be used both when bringing a new brand to market and when repositioning an existing brand, which is closely related to differentiating between products and services so that a particular brand does not become just such a cliché.

c. This is crucial given the 1990s market, where intense competition floods customers with numerous service offerings and confusing advertising messages.

d. It is a strategic tool that can be used to find answers to questions about where a particular company's current location is, where it should be moved in the future, and what to do to make this move successful.

e. It is useful for discovering opportunities in the niche market that competitors have not preoccupied. Therefore, positioning can make an important contribution to both the development of new services and the redesign of the services currently being provided.

③ The Principles of Service Positioning

a. An entity should have a position in its target customer's mind.

b. The location should be unique, providing a simple yet consistent message.

c. The position should be able to distinguish itself from other competitors.

d. One company cannot be everything to everyone. Concentrate your efforts.

④ Service Positioning Process

a. Determine positioning level

  • Industry General Positioning: Positioning at a specific service industry

  • Organizational Positioning: Positioning at the overall of a specific organization

- Service Category Positioning: Positioning for a series of service category
- Individual Service Positioning: Positioning for a particular service

b. Identifying the Key Attributes of Target Segmented Market

Once the desired level of positioning is determined, important attributes must be identified, especially those significant to specific market segments. Several situational factors influence these attributes. For instance, consumers use different criteria when choosing a restaurant based on the purpose (satisfying hunger or entertaining clients), the timing (weekday lunch or weekend dinner), and the decision-making unit (individual or group).

c. Create a Positioning Map

- After identifying important attributes, each service provider should be positioned on the positioning map. As for a product or service, a two-dimensional positioning map using two attributes that are generally considered most important to the customer is typically used.
- The positioning map can identify not only the location of the company's service but also the location of competitors' services, and by creating a more detailed positioning map for each sub-segmented market, it is possible to identify the location of each segment of the company's service. It can also find niche markets that competitors have not yet targeted, or find targets that can reposition their products and services.

Usefulness of Positioning Maps

- Understanding the concept of Niche Market
- Understanding the competitiveness position of product
- Able to determine the competitor's position
- Able to measure the effectiveness of marketing mix

d. Selection and Execution of Positioning Alternatives

- Strengthen Current Position: It is a positioning strategy alternative that sticks to current position.
- Securing a Position in an Preoccupied Market (targeting niche market): To find a gap in the market that is not preoccupied by any competitor and occupy this part.

(4) Service Differentiation – Theater Industry

① The Development and Service of CGV in Complex Movie Theater

a. Facility

The film industry, which has long been recognized as a low value-added industry, is transforming into a high value-added industry that lays golden eggs in the 21st century. The number of moviegoers per year is also approaching the era of 200 million, and high-tech complex movie theaters are also appearing one after another. However, although the number of moviegoers has increased, the phenomenon of the poor and the poor in the film industry is also intensifying. As the number of complex movie theaters armed with high-tech services and facilities has increased significantly, some movie theaters are growing rapidly as they enter the era of infinite competition, and the number of movie theaters that disappear due to their closure is also increasing. Let's look at the differentiated services of theaters based on the case of CGV, which has grown dramatically over a short period of time.

b. Overview

CGV is strengthening and implementing strategies such as establishing a system for nationwide chaining and services through the preoccupation of the optimal theater location, and using differentiated Cinema Marketing by introducing network reinforcement and CRM. In addition, as well as maximizing value and profit through the Only One strategy, it is constantly developing Only One Item such as the installation of turn ticketing machine, children's playroom, gold class, CGV lounge, natural scent air conditioning system, and powder room.

② STP Analysis of CGV Growth

a. Segmentation of Theater Industry

• Enthusiast

For consumers who want to satisfy their desire to watch movies, which is the most basic purpose of visiting movie theaters, watching movies in good facilities is the most important factor for them. It is distributed mainly among young people in their 20s and 30s because cultural experiences are important as consumers who do not simply watch movies but recognize values.

• Couples

As movie theaters are one of the most popular dating courses, consumers value attractions such as restaurants, cafes, and events along with movies. The group consists of people in their late teens and 20s.

- Family Visitors

The family-level class is not just for the purpose of watching movies, but feels the need for shopping or additional facilities that can satisfy the needs of other family members. In addition, the need for children's playrooms is increasing for the family-level demand group with children.

b. Market Targeting

- Age

The target audience for complex movie theaters is from their late teens to their 30s. This generation has quite different characteristics from the previous generation, and each generation shows unique characteristics and consumption patterns. I think the image is reflected by enjoying and feeling satisfied with not only the movie but also the movie theater itself, and furthermore, what kind of movie you watch in which place. In addition, they are reasonable consumers of cross-shopping, and at the same time, they are generations with consumption characteristics that do not consider regional aspects in order to watch movies in a good place.

- Geographical Location

When selecting a store to operate a complex movie theater, it was necessary to pay attention to whether there was sufficient purchasing power. First of all, more than 90% of movie theaters were placed in Seoul and the metropolitan area because Seoul and the metropolitan area have a larger number of purchasing populations than local cities.

c. Positioning

• Value

CGV, which introduced complex movie theaters, was differentiated from existing movie theaters by giving them clear cultural value for the first time in domestic movie theaters. By branding movie theaters with one-stop entertainment, advanced facilities, and high services, it pioneered a differentiated market called complex movie theaters-CGV.

• pleasant facilities and luxurious atmosphere

With the philosophy of "Movie theaters should impress more than movies", it was intended to increase consumers' satisfaction with surrounding services as well as the enjoyment of watching movies through a luxurious atmosphere and convenient facility arrangement differentiated from existing movie theaters.

③ CGV's Differentiated Services

a. One-stop Entertainment

Instead of thinking of a movie theater as a place where people only watch movies, it introduced early morning, which prioritized customer benefits, movie screening hours until late at night, and various movie ticket reservation methods such as the Internet, phone, and mobile phones. In addition, separate facilities and services were provided for disabled people to watch movies, and parking services were strengthened.

b. All-new-one

The glass barrier at the ticket office was removed to ease the audience's unwillingness, and all ticket agents were raised and decorated like a hotel front to make the desk comfortable for customers and employees to talk.

In addition, the Internet reservation system has been greatly reinforced to minimize waiting time.

c. Service recall system

If a customer who has received unsatisfactory service while visiting a theater to watch a movie makes a reasonable complaint, the customer is invited to an unopened movie premiere for free. This system provided an opportunity to manage dissatisfied customers to improve service, enhance brand image, and correct mistakes and rearmament with the spirit of service.

④ Only One Strategy

a. Golden Class

Some CGV theaters operate Gold Class, a luxury theater that looks like the first class of aircraft has been moved for those who want to comfortably watch movies. In a general theater, a 30-seat wide and fluffy luxury sofa is installed in the space that will hold 200 seats. This seat is a bed-type sofa that can be tilted back up to 120 degrees, so you can watch movies while lying down and enjoying drinks and meals such as wine, juice, and beer, and watch movies like aristocrats.

b. Children's playroom

CGV Yatap runs a children's playroom for free only for infants aged 2 to 4 who are not allowed to enter general movie theaters, breaking the conventional wisdom that "when they have a baby, they are done watching movies". The operating hours are from the start of the first movie to 10 o'clock. In the playroom, an indoor theater system is established on a large screen, so they select videos exclusively for infants that have educational value or can foster children's imagination.

c. CGV Lounge service for VIP customers

When excellent customers wait with movie time left, they have a resting place such as an airport VIP room. Through this service, excellent customer management is performed by giving customers the perception that 'I am being treated differently'.

d. Mobile ticket service

In the time, service that allows users not only to book movie tickets but also to directly buy tickets has appeared on the market. CGV boasts a unique system called "Cell Phone Ticketing Service". This is a method of completing authentication without a separate ticket with the digital barcode displayed on the mobile phone's terminal window. The user can pay the fees by credit card or mobile phone micro payment system. The user can save and use multiple tickets, transfer them to someone else's phone, or gift the ticket.

6.2 · Analysis of Customer

(1) Application of Customer Psychology

① Attraction Effect : If a company has a major brand that it wants to grow, it will release a relatively inferior new brand to increase the consumer's chances of choosing the main brand

② Part-list Cunning Effect : Since people only remember the first place and not the second and third places, the message is that they will have a showdown between the first and second places

③ Compromise Effect : Putting the main brand in the middle is safe when selling products in multiple price ranges.

④ The Principle of Scarcity : Choose a good or service that will provide greater satisfaction because not everything can be attained.

(2) Degree of Involvement

① Degree of Involvement refers to the level to which a person perceives relevance or importance to an object, and is classified into high involvement and low involvement according to the intensity of interest in the object, the degree of interest, and personal importance.

② The level of consumer involvement depends on the characteristics of the product, the characteristics of the consumer, the usage situation, and marketing communication. For example, in the case of expensive products such as cars and computers, consumer involvement increases, and in the case of low-cost products such as detergents and ballpoint pens, the involvement decreases.

③ When the degree of involvement is high, consumers are active in acquiring product information, making active efforts, and contemplating purchasing decisions.

④ If the degree of involvement is low, the product information becomes passive, and the purchase is decided based on repeated information remembered by advertisements or promotions.

⑤ Degree of involvement can be divided into situational involvement and continuous involvement depending on the circumstances in which it is involved, and situational involvement occurs in a particular situation, and continuous involvement refers to a relatively long-term involvement in a product of interest.

(3) Customer Analysis Techniques

① RFM Analysis Technique

It is a method of analyzing a customer's rating based on three factors: Recency (when to purchase), Frequency (how often to purchase), and Monetary (how much to purchase a product). Each factor is scored and the customer's value is evaluated based on this. Therefore, different marketing plans are made according to the customer's value and strategies are created to promote purchases.

② AIO Analysis Technique

Different scholars have different arguments, but it is one of the lifestyle measurement methods that are generally identified by Activities, Interests, and Opinions. When investigating lifestyle using AIO items, more advantageous information can be obtained by including demographic variables such as income, family life patterns, and education level.

6.3 ⟶ Understanding and Managing Customer Experience

(1) Customer Experience(CE)

It refers to the impression that a customer feels during their interactions with products, services, and companies. This can happen either directly or indirectly, from the information search stage before making a purchase to the purchase and use stages. In other words, sensory information is added and recognized throughout these interactions.

(2) Customer Experience Management (CEM)

① Definition: CEM is a process that measures and analyzes consumer experiences as they occur in real-time at all points of contact between companies and consumers. It involves gathering and reflecting these insights in the development of products and services. This approach enables companies to create strategies and methods for enhancing consumer experiences.

② Importance of Customer Experience Management

a. Customers' desire for experience consumption is growing. Customers are no longer willing to pay only for the features or benefits of the product. They value the unique lifestyle and overall experience gained by using products more.

b. The quality of experience is influencing the performance of a company. Recently, many companies try to sell experiences that are not at the level of products and services.

example) Eric Schmidt, CEO of Google, an Internet search company, emphasized, "Our outstanding performance is the result of a dramatic improvement in the quality of the user experience".

c. Customer experience management is highly utilized as a complementary means of customer relationship management (CRM).

③ Customer Experience Management Success Process

a. Step 1: Dissect the customer's experience process

In order for a company to perform customer experience management, above all, it is necessary to thoroughly understand the customer's world of experience.

- The customer's world of experience is divided into three dimensions: product and service, communication, and people.
- Companies should clearly define the target customer's experience factors by identifying customer contacts in the entire purchase. The process should be based on the three dimensions of experience.

b. Step 2: Design a differentiated experience

If a company accurately analyzes the customer's world of experience, it should create a differentiated experience compared to its competitors.

- Prioritize experience by identifying differences between customer expectations and actual experiences for each of the three dimensions of experience, identifying satisfaction and dissatisfaction factors
- Based on priorities and Unique Selling Experience (USE), a combination of unique selling experiences

c. Step 3: Reflect customer feedback

Companies should actively reflect the evaluation of their customers' opinions and experiences.

- Engage customers to increase effectiveness and attractiveness to unique sales experiences
- Firms actively reflect customer feedback to build their consensus

d. Step 4: Provide a consistent and integrated experience

An entity should use it to increase customer value by providing a consistent and integrated experience to customers.

- Comprehensive management of quality of experience within the enterprise to provide consistent customer experience through a variety of contacts
- If a consistent experience is not provided, the experience at various points of contact may become noisy, and the company's intended delivery of the brand message may fail.

| Customer Experience Management (CEM) execution process |

(3) Best Practices of Customer Experience

Customer experience analysis is the starting point and most important element of CEM. In order to analyze customer experience, it is necessary to deeply understand what actual customers are experiencing through customer research, as well as to observe and investigate cases that provide excellent customer experiences.

① Brand Promise

CEM is also an expression of a company's willingness to deliver a certain experience to customers, which is called Brand Promise. In other words, customer experience management refers to a series of activities that manage and monitor activities at all points of contact so that customers can have a positive experience, but among them, communication is necessary to accurately recognize discriminatory characteristics to customers. This is what Brand Promise becomes.

The 7 Customer Promises of the UK mobile carrier O2
• Provide the best device lineup
• Ensure reliable network quality
• Deliver worthwhile services
• Employ considerate staff
• Offer easy-to-use products/services
• Offer great value
• Provide an excellent shopping environment

② Branded CEM : It means to create a brand based on customer experience analysis through CEM.

Starbucks: The brand image or in-store experience that customers think of when they hear 'Starbucks' has become a unique characteristic of the company.

6.4 Customer Value Proposition (Personalization) Strategy

(1) Customer Value

① Definition

Customer Value = Total Customer Benefits - Total Customer Cost

Customer value can generally be defined as the difference between a set of benefits that a customer expects from a particular product or service and the total cost that they will pay. The benefits that customers expect from a product or service minus the total costs such as money, time, and effort that customers incur to evaluate, acquire, and use that product or service. After all, one of the good ways a company can satisfy its customers' needs is to provide products that give customers higher value than their competitors.

a. Customer value before use and customer value after use
- Customer value before product use refers to the value of the what customers expect before purchasing a product.
- Customer value after product use is process-oriented value felt after use. Experience, integration, classification, and society fall under this category.

b. Explicit customer value and implicit customer value
- Explicit customer value refers to the value that consumers share about the tangible quality of a product or service.
- Implicit customer value refers to a unique intangible personal value.

c. The customer value from the customer's perspective and company perspective

- Customer value is how customers perceive the benefits they receive from a company's offer after subtracting the costs they incur to get it. It is also called customer perception value or customer delivery value. Customer perception of value is relative because it changes from one customer to another and is influenced by how it compares to competitor's value propositions.

- From a company point of view, customer value measures how much a particular customer can pay for a product or service from a long-term perspective, and is also called lifelong customer value.

② Creating Customer Value

a. The formation of cyclical relationships with values

- Value for customers: Companies focus on delivering services that customers desire, rather than offering services dictated solely by the company

- Customer Value: Develop a customer who is valuable to the company

- Value by customers: Make customers naturally increase the value of the company.

b. Changing the perception of companies to create value for customers

- The customer only requests the service the company promised to provide. Therefore, the primary responsibility for not satisfying customers lies with the company.

- Customers do not want to be treated as kings, but rather as corporate partners. They are satisfied with the product that has solved the problems they pointed out and reflects their opinions, and are willing to purchase it.

- It's impossible to satisfy all customers. Missing out on valuable customers who dont reciprocate as much as the company did is not ideal, and having many customers isn't necessarily beneficial.

- First of all, the customer must be able to truly feel comfortable at each contact point they directly or indirectly encounter with the company. To do so, it is necessary to continue paying attention to the customer itself, not the sales situation.

③ The Type of Value the Customer is Pursuing (Karl Albrecht)

a. Step 1 (Basic value)

- It is the primary value for customers to find a company.

- It is an absolute value that must be equipped with when a product or service is provided, and if it is not provided, the customer will refuse to choose.

- For example, hospitals refer to the perfect quality of competent medical staff, facilities, and automobiles.

b. Step 2 (Expected Value)

- Customers want all the procedures and systems of the company to be convenient.

- It is a value that customers naturally expect and believe will be provided. The important thing is that if it is not provided, it will be a factor that will offend (unsatisfied).

- For example, if its an airplane, it leaves at a fixed time and arrives on time.

c. Step 3 (Desired Value)

- It's not necessarily expected to be provided, but the desired value is expressed internally.

- For example, hospitals serve warm tea to waiting patients in winter, or banks give gifts to customers when they sign up for installment savings.

d. Step 4 (Unknown Value, Unexpected Value)

- It refers to the value that is unexpectedly provided to customers beyond the level of expectation or wish and gives impression and joy.

- Because it 'impresses customers', it is a value that realizes customer satisfaction beyond customer satisfaction.

- For example, when a patient who has been treated in the morning calls a hospital in the afternoon and asks if there is any inconvenience, or when a car center distributes winter winter equipment to customers for free.

e. Conclusion

- Basic and expected values must be understood and fully equipped before starting a business.

- Desired and unexpected values are values to win the competition, and how to identify and differentiate the desired and unexpected values pursued by customers is the shortcut to business success or failure and competitive advantage and survival strategy.

- Customers sometimes want the value they demand to be created and provided, verbally and sometimes unconsciously. After all, it is the way for companies to recognize their status to actively cope with the various values sought by customers.

(2) Personalization strategy

① Concept

    a. The personalization strategy is an activity that increases the business value of a company by providing information suitable for the characteristics and preferences of individual customers based on the needs of customers.

    b. It is a system designed to increase customer satisfaction through community engagement. This involves identifying customer needs using various information gathered through communication with them. The system efficiently processes internal data and information based on individual customers' areas of interest and characteristics.

② Purpose

The personalization strategy aims to maximize the satisfaction of customer service by building relationships through constant communication with customers.

③ 'Customer Occupancy' and 'Conversations with Customers'

    a. 'Share of Customer' contrasts with 'Share of Market'. While market share focuses on selling a specific product on a large scale in a homogeneous market, customer share emphasizes identifying each customer's unique needs. It aims to encourage customers to continue purchasing by meeting their needs and highlighting the importance of 'Customer Value'.

    b. Through 'dialogue with customers', it becomes possible to understand exactly what the customers' needs are and predict how these will change. This enables companies to provide products and services that better suit their customers and to develop new products and services by identifying customer needs.

④ Expectation Effect

    a. By providing differentiated services, it increases customer loyalty and enables us to extract valuable superior customers by considering current and future profitability among existing customers in terms of customer management.

    b. By focusing marketing capabilities on customers, it is possible to reduce costs and increase sales.

    c. The word of mouth effect on superior customers affects securing new customers.

    d. It affects strengthening competitiveness by continuously improving products and services, increasing customer loyalty, classifying customers, reducing marketing costs, and improving services and products.

Additional Information
Additional Information!

- Expected effects of personalization strategy in e-business
- Increase customer loyalty through differentiated customer management
- Increase work efficiency and reduce costs through automation of marketing processes
- Increase strategic customer value
- Building strategies and accumulating customer management know-how for various companies

⑤ Examples of Personalization Strategies

    a. Personalized service using the web and e-mail of Ford and GM: It effectively uses customer information in connection with offline car exhibition halls and test driving programs.

    b. An online shopping mall called Cabela's, which sells outdoor products: membership services and newsletter services provide a variety of information about customers.

Service Quality

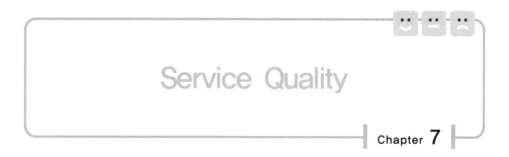

Service Quality

Chapter **7**

Concept of Service Quality

(1) Definition of Service Quality

Service quality, being intangible compared to the quality of products or goods, has few measurable tangible indicators. Consequently, the tangible aspects of service quality are confined to the physical capabilities or human elements of the service provider. Therefore, service quality is defined as a perception recognized by the consumer based on subjective criteria.

Sasser et al. (1978)[18] stated that the method of service delivery, including aspects such as materials, facilities, and personnel involved in the service process, is also part of service quality.

---

18) Sasser, W. E., Olsen, R. P., Wyckoff, D. D., & of Business Administration, H. U. G. S. (1978). *Management of Service Operations: Text, Cases, and Readings.* Allyn and Bacon.

Lewis & Booms (1983)[19] defined service quality as the extent to which the delivered service matches customer expectations, emphasizing that service quality involves consistently providing services that meet these expectations.

Research on service quality includes Lehinen's (1983)[20] perspective, Service Quality: A Study of Quality Dimensions', Service Management Institute. This perspective posits that service quality is determined by three dimensions: first, the interaction between consumers and elements within the service organization; second, the physical quality; and third, the corporate quality. Subsequently, service quality was initially defined by conceptualizing it into two dimensions: process quality and outcome quality.

Meanwhile, service quality can be evaluated differently by every consumers, even for the same service, due to their different perspectives. Therefore, it is assessed through a multidimensional evaluation rather than a single-dimensional evaluation.

Grönroos (1984)[21] formally introduced the concept of perceived service quality by distinguishing it into technical quality and functional quality, aiming to measure services from the consumer's perceived perspective. Following this, Parasuraman, Zeithaml, and Berry (1998) defined service quality as the difference between customers' expectations of the service provided by the service firm and their perceptions of the actual service received. In 1985[22], through focus group interviews, they identified ten dimensions of service quality determinants. However,

19) Lewis, R. C., & Booms, B. H. (1983). The Marketing Aspects of Service Quality. In L. L. Berry, G. Shostack, & G. Upah (Eds.), *Emerging Perspectives on Services Marketing*. American Marketing Association.

20) Lehtinen, U. (1982). *Service Quality: A Study of Quality Dimensions*. Service Management Institute.

21) Grönroos, C. (1984). A Service Quality Model and its Marketing Implications. European Journal of Marketing, 18(4), 36-44.

22) Parasuraman, A., Zeithaml, V. A., & Berry, L. L. (1985). A Conceptual Model of Service Quality and Its Implications for Future Research. *Journal of Marketing, 49*(4), 41-50.

not all these factors were independent. To enhance empirical validity and develop a measurement scale, they revised the dimensions in 1988[23] to five: tangibles, reliability, responsiveness, assurance, and empathy.

① Tangibiles: Physical facilities, equipment, personnel, and communication tools

② Reliability: The ability to perform the promised service dependably and accurately

③ Responsiveness: The willingness to help customers and provide prompt service

④ Assurance: The employees' knowledge and courtesy, and their ability to inspire trust and confidence

⑤ Empathy: The ability to provide caring, individualized attention to customers

Therefore, PZB (1998) defined service quality as subjective rather than objective quality and made three proposals:

First, service quality is more difficult for customers to evaluate than product quality.

Second, the perception of service quality is determined by comparing customer expectations with the actual service performance.

Third, quality evaluation includes not only the outcome of the service but also the service delivery process.

---

23) Parasuraman, A., Berry, L. L., Zeithaml, V. A., Kelley, S. W., & Turley, L. W. (1988). SERVQUAL: A Multiple-Item Scale for Measuring Consumer Perceptions of Service Quality. *Journal of Retailing, 64*(1), 12–40.

Service quality is influenced by a complex interplay of various factors such as the characteristics of the service, consumer expectations, and the complexity of evaluation criteria, making it difficult to define the concept with a single definition. However, researchers and managers of service companies agree that service quality is related to the gap between expectations and performance.

As many companies globalize, the quality of the service industry has rapidly improved. At a time when the service industry holds a significant share of the national economy, ongoing research in the service sector highlights that the issue of service quality is not merely a matter for private enterprises to meet diverse customer needs and changes.

Service quality is defined based on a user-centered perspective, where it is determined by the unique characteristics of the service. It is specifically defined as the perceived service quality, which results from the comparison between the customer's perceived service performance and their expected service.

| Definition of Service Quality |

Researcher	Definition
Grönross (1984)	Service quality is defined as the consumer perception based on the comparison between the customer's perceived actual service performance and their prior expectations of the service
Zeithaml (1988)[24]	Service quality is defined as the customer's evaluation of the overall superiority or excellence of the service.
PZB (1998)	Service quality is defined as the consumer's judgment regarding the overall excellence or superiority of a particular service, which is a form of attitude distinct from objective quality
Bitner & Hubbert (1944)[25]	Service quality is defined as the consumer's overall impression of the relative inferiority or superiority of the organization and its services

| Perspectives on Service Quality |

Service quality can be broadly defined from two main perspectives: the customer needs perspective and the customer perceived quality perspective.

The customer needs perspective focuses on service quality in terms of how well the provided service meets the customer's requirements and needs, emphasizing the extent to which the service meets customer expectations and demands. In contrast, the customer perceived quality perspective views service quality based on the expectation-disconfirmation paradigm, defining it as the perceived difference between customer expectations and actual performance.

However, since service quality comprises various attributes, simply meeting one of the many relevant quality attributes does not fully address customer needs. Thus, the customer needs perspective has been criticized as a flawed concept (Chatterjee and Yilmaz, 1933)[26]. Recently, the customer perceived quality perspective, based on the expectation-disconfirmation paradigm, has gained significant support in the academic community.

(2) Characteristics of Service Quality

Service quality traditionally encompasses characteristics of both objective quality and subjective quality perceived by consumers. However, Holbrook and Coffman (1985)[27] introduced the concepts of mechanistic quality and humanistic quality instead of using the term "quality". Mechanistic quality includes the objective aspects and features of things or events, while humanistic quality reflects people's

---

24) Zeithaml, V. A. (1988). Consumer Perceptions of Price, Quality, and Value: A Means-End Model and Synthesis of Evidence. *Journal of Marketing*, 52(3), 2–22.

25) Bitner, M. J., & Hubbert, A. R. (1994). Encounter Satisfaction versus Overall Satisfaction versus Quality: The Customer's Voice. In R. T. Rust & R. L. Oliver (Eds.), *Service Quality: New Directions in Theory and Practice* (pp. 72–94). Thousand Oaks, CA: Sage.

26) Chatterjee, S., & Yilmaz, M. (1993). Quality Confusion: Too Many Gurus, Not Enough Disciples. *Business Horizons, 36*(3), 15–18.

27) Holbrook, M. B., & Corfman, K. P. (1985). Quality and Value in the Consumption Experience: Phaedrus Rides Again. In J. Jacoby & J. C. Olson (Eds.), *Perceived Quality: How Consumers View and Merchandise* (pp. 31–57). Lexington Books.

subjective responses to objects.

Additionally, Garvin (1984)[28] proposed five approaches to understanding quality as follows.

① Transcendent Approach

Quality is difficult to define precisely and has characteristics that are not easily analyzed; it can only be recognized through experience. In other words, humans can perceive quality through continuous experience.

② Product-based approach

Quality is understood as an exact and measurable variable, where differences in quality are viewed from the objective perspective of differences in the contents and attributes of the product. Therefore, it has the weak point of not accounting for the subjective tastes, needs, or preferences of consumers.

③ User-based Approach

Quality is defined with customer satisfaction from the customer's perspective, reflecting intentional quality differences to meet various customer needs and desires. Therefore, performance, size, and features of the product must be considered during the design phase.

④ Manufacturing-based Approach

Quality is supplier-oriented and viewed from an engineering perspective, where producers evaluate quality based on conformance to requirements or conformance to specifications. This is referred to as the quality of conformance, and it is determined by various fixed factors such as personnel, materials, and equipment.

---

28) Garvin, D. A. (1984). What Does Product Quality Really Mean? *Sloan Management Review, 26*(1), 25-43.

⑤ Value-based Approach

Quality is defined in the two dimensions of value and price, which corresponds to the concept of cost-effectiveness. This means that a high-quality product is one that offers suitability at a satisfactory price.

These various perspectives on service quality are not mutually exclusive but rather complementary. Each perspective is valuable and offers significant insights for the study of service quality, making it desirable to consider them together.

(3) Reasons for Measuring Service Quality

① Starting point for improvement, enhancement, and redesign.

② Increasing importance of service quality in securing competitive advantage.

(4) Challenges in Measuring Service Quality

① Because the concept of service quality is subjective, it is difficult to objectify and measure it, and defining a service quality standard that applies to all cases is challenging.

② Service quality is difficult to verify before the delivery of the service is complete. This is because, due to the nature of services, production and consumption occur simultaneously.

③ To measure service quality, it is necessary to understand customers' perceptions of quality. Collecting data from customers is time-consuming and costly, and response rates are often low.

④ When resources move along with the customer during the service delivery process, customers can observe the flow of resources. This can undermine the objectivity of measuring service quality.

⑤ Customers are part of the service process and can be a significant factor in causing variations. Therefore, there are inherent difficulties in researching and measuring service quality that targets customers.

(5) Reasons for Low Service Quality

| Factors for Low Quality in the Service Industry |

Category	Content
Cost Reduction	• Difficult to expect high-quality service in restaurants with fewer staff to reduce labor costs • Expansion of self-service and automation due to rising labor costs (customer confusion and insufficient employee training). • Replacing labor with machines reduces customer-facing staff, leading to lower service quality
Perception of the Service Industry	• Many people consider it a temporary job to stay in and then leave • Perception that jobs done by service workers are unskilled and require no training • Low motivation
Gap in Productivity and Efficiency	• Emphasis on productivity and efficiency in services leads to compromised service quality Example) ① In a call center, setting a fixed time for phone consultations and using a buzzer to signal if the call exceeds the allotted time ② To meet the rule of answering the phone before the third ring, staff might quickly pick up and hang up the call without assisting the customer
Lack of Awareness of Customer Satisfaction	• Customers often assume that the service level will not be high and therefore do not make additional demands • Service providers mistakenly believe their service is satisfying customers (only 4 out of 100 dissatisfied customers actually voice their complaints)

Difficulty in Standardiz ation	• Services provided to a large number of customers often have a higher likelihood of errors due to the nature of the service • Compared to product manufacturing, standardizing service production is challenging, and there are few ways to inspect quality before the service is delivered to the customer • Many customers have had unsatisfactory service experiences in places with a large customer base, such as banks or department stores
Intangible Nature of Services	• Services occur simultaneously with production, leaving few methods for quality control • Service providers produce intangible services, so quality must be measured based on opinions, perceptions, or expectations of the intangible service • Many believe that intangibility means it cannot be quantified, and if it cannot be quantified, it cannot be measured or controlled

7.2 Determinants of Service Quality

(1) Research on Service Quality

Research on the dimensions that constitute service quality is fundamental for measuring and improving service quality. Existing literature on this topic can be broadly divided into three approaches.

① Two-Dimensional Approach: Research by Grönroos (1983)[29], Berry (1985)[30]

---

29) Grönroos, C. (1983). Innovative Marketing Strategies and Organization Structures for Services Firms. In Lovelock (Ed.), *Services Marketing: Text, Cases and Readings* (pp. 433‒448). Prentice Hall International Editions.

30) Berry, L. L., Zeithaml, V. A., & Parasuraman, A. (1985). Quality Counts in Services, too. *Business Horizons*, 28(3), 44‒52.

② Three-Dimensional Model of Service Quality: **Research by Lehtinen & Lehtinen (1991)**[31] **and Karmarkar & Pitbladdo (1993)**[32]

③ Multidimensional Determinants of Service Quality: **Research by Parasuraman (1985)**[33] **Johnstone (1990)**[34]

| Comparison of Studies on Service Quality Dimensions |

Category	Researcher	Content
Two-Dimensional Approach	Grönroos(1983)	Technical Quality, Functional Quality
	Berry et al.(1985)	Outcome Quality, Process Quality
Three-Dimensional Model	Lehtinen(1991)	Physical Quality, Interaction Quality, Corporate (Image) Quality
	Karmarkar & Pitbladdo (1993)	Performance Quality, Conformance Quality, Communication Quality
Multidimensional Determinants PZB	Parasuraman et al.(1985)	Reliability, Tangibles, Responsiveness, Assurance, Empathy
	Johnston et al.(1990)	Accessibility, Aesthetics, Attention/Assistance, Availability, Consideration, Cleanliness/Tidiness, Comfort, Engagement, Communication, Competence, Courtesy, Functionality, Friendliness, Flexibility, Integrity, Trust, Responsiveness, Safety

31) Lehtinen, U., & Lehtinen, J. R. (1991). Two Approaches to Service Quality Dimensions. *The Service Industries Journal, 11*(3), 287-303.

32) Karmarkar, U. S., & Pitbladdo, R. C. (1997). Quality, Class, and Competition. *Management Science, 43*(1), 27-39.

33) Parasuraman, A., Zeithaml, V. A., & Berry, L. L. (1985). A Conceptual Model of Service Quality and Its Implications for Future Research. *Journal of Marketing, 49*(4), 41-50.

34) Johnston, R., Silvestro, R., Fitzgerald, L., & Voss, C. (1990). Developing the determinants of service quality. In Proceedings of the *1st International Research Seminar in Service Management*. La Londes les Maures, France.

| Trends in Service Quality Research |

Physical quality, Synergy Quality, Image Quality

Technical Quality, Functional Quality

Performance Quality, Suitability Quality, Communication Quality

Service Quality Factors Research

SERVQUAL Model (Reliability, Responsiveness, Assurance, Empathy, Tangibles)

Access, Depth, Interest, Help, Warmth, Flexibility, Cleaning, Neatness, Convenience, Objects, Communication, Role, Friendliness, Functionality, Familiarity, Naturalness, Loyalty, Trust, Response, Safety

(2) Service Quality Measurement Models

① SERVQUAL

SERVQUAL is a term combining "Service" and "Quality" and is a representative concept for explaining the dimensions of service quality. It is characterized by its development of a scale to measure service quality based on the comparison between consumers' expectations and their perceptions of the actual service.

It defines service quality as the difference between customers' perceptions of a specific company's service and their expectations of the service provider. It identifies 10 dimensions as evaluation factors for service quality, with 97 items representing these dimensions, which are used to measure expectations and perceptions.

SERVQUAL is a service quality measurement tool developed by PZB in the United States. It is a multiple-item scale that service companies can use to understand customer expectations and evaluations.

Initially, extensive literature reviews and exploratory research on service quality were conducted, which involved forming 12 customer groups for focus group interviews. The focus group interviews were conducted in four service sectors: banking, credit card companies, securities companies, and product repair companies. Three groups were formed for each sector, leading to the following conclusions.

a. Definition of Service Quality: The results of the focus group interviews clearly indicate that excellent service quality means meeting or exceeding customer expectations. In other words, service quality as perceived by customers is defined as the extent of the difference between their expectations or desires and their actual perceptions of the service.

b. Factors Affecting Expectations: The key factors contributing to the formation of customer expectations include word-of-mouth, individual desires of customers, past experiences with the service, and external communications from the service provider.

c. Dimensions of Service Quality: The 10 common and general criteria used by customers to evaluate service quality are as follows.

| Customer Evaluation of Service Quality |

• Tangibles
- Physical cues for evaluating the service
- Example: Appearance of physical facilities, equipment, staff, and materials

• Credibility
- The ability to perform the promised service dependably and accurately
- Example: Timeliness of service, immediate response to customer inquiries or requests, quick service delivery

• Responsiveness
- Willingness to help customers and provide prompt service
- Example: Timeliness of service, immediate response to customer inquiries or requests, quick service delivery

• Competence
- Possession of necessary skills and knowledge to perform the service
- Example: Research and development capabilities of the organization, knowledge and skills of staff and support personnel

• Courtesy
- Politeness, respect, consideration, and friendliness of frontline staff
- Example: Consideration for customer' property and time, polite behavior of staff

• Trustworthiness
- The reliability and honesty of the service provider
- Example: Company reputation, brand name, employee honesty, degree of hard-selling

• Reliability
- Ease of reaching and using the service
- Example: Convenience of contact methods, minimal waiting times, and accessible service locations

• Safety
- Absence of risks or concerns
- Example: Physical safety, financial security, and confidentiality

• Communication
- Clear and effective communication with customers
- Example: Providing understandable explanations of services and costs, and addressing customer concerns

• Customer Understanding
- Efforts to understand and cater to customer needs
- Example: Personalized attention, understanding specific customer requirements, and recognizing loyal customers

Service Quality Evaluation	SERVQUAL Dimension	Definition of SERVQUAL Dimension
Tangibles	Tangibles	Appearance of physical facilities, equipment, personnel, and communication materials
Credibility	Reliability	Ability to perform the promised service dependably and accurately
Responsiveness	Responsiveness	Willingness to help customers and provide prompt service
Assurance	Assurance	Ability to convey trust and confidence through the knowledge and courtesy of employees
Courtesy		
Reliability		
Safety		
Accessibility	Empathy	Individual attention and care provided by the company to customers
Communication		
Customer Understanding		

② Relative Importance of Service Quality Determinants

Reliability > Responsiveness > Assurance > Tangibles > Empathy (with a focus on outcomes)

③ Service Quality Gap Model

After developing SERVQUAL to measure customer perceptions of service quality through exploratory research and empirical studies, the next phase focused on internal factors affecting service quality. This led to creating a conceptual model that links customer-perceived quality issues with internal shortcomings or gaps within the organization.

| Service Quality Gap Model |

Service quality is determined by Gap 5, which is influenced by Gaps 1 through 4.

- **Gap 1** : [Expected Service – Management's Perception of Customer Expectations] - Management Perception Gap
- **Gap 2** : [Management's Perception of Quality Specifications - Management's Perception of Customer Expectations] - Management Specification Gap
- **Gap 3** : [Service Delivery - Quality Specifications Perceived by Management] - Service Delivery Gap
- **Gap 4** : [Service Delivery - External Communication to Customers] - Market Communication Gap
- **Gap 5** : [Expected Service - Perceived Service] - Experienced Service Gap and Service Quality Gap Model

| Definition of gap factors |

Gap	Factor	Definition
Gap 1	Marketing Research Orientation	• The extent to which managers strive to understand customer needs and expectations through formal and informal information collection • Occurs due to the use of insufficient or inadequate marketing research results or a lack of interaction between management and customers
	Upward Communication	• The extent to which top management promotes, stimulates, and seeks information flow from employees • Occurs when customer demands do not reach top management
	Management Levels	• Differences based on the number of management levels between the top and bottom • Management levels restrict communication and mutual understanding between managers who set actual standards and employees who execute them • Information gets omitted or distorted, and customer expectations are not properly communicated
Gap 2	Managerial Commitment to	• The extent to which management prioritizes service quality as a core strategic goal

	Service Quality	• Many companies often align with internal standards for quality but fail to meet customer expectations
	Perceived Possibility	• The extent to which managers believe they can meet customer expectations • The perception of impossibility can be overcome through service innovation • Creating possibilities is crucial instead of perceiving limitations
	Tasks Standardization	• The extent to which technology can be used to standardize service tasks • Standardization is the best method for maximizing efficiency • In repetitive services, tasks can be standardized through specific procedures or regulations, even specialized services requiring customization can apply standardization to some tasks
	Goal Achievement	• The extent to which service quality goals are set based on customer standards
Gap 3	Role Ambiguity	• The extent of unawareness regarding the unclear expectations of managers or superiors and how to meet the expectations • Occurs when insufficient information or training makes job performance difficult • Employees do not know their own expectations or how their performance is measured and evaluated
	Role Conflict	• Occurs when employees are unable to satisfy all the demands from everyone they interact with (internal and external customers) or when they are required to handle tasks quickly while managing dual roles with customers
	Employee-Job Fit	• The harmony between employees' skills and their job roles • Occurs due to a mismatch between employee skills and job requirements • Often, lower-paid employees handle customer contact roles, and when management is indifferent to job fit, problems arise. Addressing these issues may involve team discussions or enhancing relationships through club activities
	Technology-Job Fit	• The harmony between the equipment and technology used by employees during job performance

		• Provides assistance when tools or technologies needed for job performance are inadequate
	Supervision and Control Systems	• The adequacy of evaluation and reward systems • Concerns about the appropriateness of evaluation and rewards within the company • Service employees' performance is often controlled by behavioral control systems, though many measure performance based on quantitative service outcomes
	Perceived Authority in Decision-making	• The extent to which employees perceive they can exercise flexibility in dealing with issues encountered during service provision • Low when organizational regulations, procedures, or culture restrict resource flexibility or decision-making authority is beyond scope • Empowering employees involves trusting them and giving them authority to represent the organization, rather than relying on mechanical and standardized methods
	Teamwork	• The extent of effort towards shared goals between employees and management • Strong commitment to the organization tends to persist if management shows interest, necessitating support and recognition of employees' efforts
Gap 4	Horizontal Communication	• The extent of communication between different departments within a company and within each department • Caused by differences in procedures and regulations between HR, marketing, and operations departments • It is advisable to first establish communication channels and check the feasibility of advertising promises made by the operations department
	Tendency for Overpromising	• The extent to which external communication by the company does not accurately reflect the service received by customers • Customers generally expect what is promised through advertising or promotions, but companies should only promise what they can deliver and strive to exceed expectations

④ Garvin's Quality Model (1984)

Garvin presented eight dimensions of quality that consider both the producer's and the user's perspectives.

| Garvin's 8 Dimensions of Quality |

Category	Concept
Performance	The operational characteristics of a product
Features	The competitive differentiation of a product
Reliability	The degree of the likelihood of failure or malfunction
Conformance	The ability to meet customers'specific needs
Durability	The period during which the product continuously provides value to the customer
Service Delivery Capability	The ability to provide speed, friendliness, problem-solving, etc
Aesthetics	The aesthetic function of appearance
Perceived Quality	The reputation of the company or brand

⑤ Grönroos's Quality Model

Grönroos defines service quality as the overall quality perceived by customers, which is determined by comparing expected service with perceived service. This model emphasizes that the quality of a service is evaluated based on how well it meets or exceeds customer expectations, and this perception is influenced by both the technical outcome of the service and the process through which it is delivered.

| Grönroos's 6 Dimensions of Quality |

Component	Content
Expertise and Skills	The customer's perception that the service provider, employees, operational systems, and physical resources possess the knowledge and skills necessary to solve their problems using professional methods
Attitudes and Behavior	The customer's feeling that employees who interact with them are friendly, willingly pay attention, and actively resolve issues
Accessibility and Flexibility	The customer's perception that the location of the service provider, service institution, employees, and operational systems are conveniently situated and designed to be adaptable to customer expectations and demands
Reliability and Trust	The customer's belief that the service provider and operational systems will consistently honor their promises and prioritize the customer in delivering services, regardless of circumstances
Service Recovery	The customer's perception that the service provider actively and promptly attempts to correct service failures or unforeseen issues and finds solutions to resolve them
Reputation and Credibility	The customer's belief that the service provider's operations are trustworthy, that the service charges are justified, and that the service's performance and value are recognized and agreed upon by both the customer and the service provider

⑥ Kano Model

a. Attractive Quality Elements

These are quality factors that exceed customer expectations or fulfill unexpected needs, providing a level of satisfaction beyond what customers anticipated. These elements can act as differentiators, helping to secure customers and gain a competitive edge. As customer expectations increase, these elements can eventually shift to become One-Dimensional or Basic Elements. This phenomenon is known as the "declining novelty effect".

b. One—Dimensional Quality Elements

These are explicit requirements from customers where satisfaction increases as these elements are fulfilled and dissatisfaction grows as they are not met. Similar to Attractive Quality Elements, as customer expectations rise, these elements can evolve into Basic Quality Elements.

c. Basic Quality Elements

These are fundamental quality factors that customers expect to be present. They do not provide additional satisfaction when fulfilled, as they are considered a given. However, their absence can lead to dissatisfaction. Therefore, they are also referred to as "dissatisfiers".

d. Indifferent Quality Elements

These are quality factors that neither increase nor decrease satisfaction regardless of whether they are present or not. They do not impact customer satisfaction significantly.

e. Reverse Quality Elements

These are quality factors that when its not fulfilled, lead to satisfaction, but when fulfilled, cause dissatisfaction. The presence of these elements can lead to mixed reactions among customers.

7.3 ⌐ Strategies for Improving Service Quality

(1) Sources of Service Quality Issues

① Inseparability of Production and Consumption, and Labor Intensity

a. Due to the inseparability of production and consumption, products are manufactured, then sold and consumed, while services are produced in the presence of the customer after being sold.

b. Due to the labor-intensive nature of services, standardization is difficult, and variations in the provided service can lead to customer dissatisfaction.

② Inadequate Service from Service Employees

a. The quality of service experienced by customers depends on the quality of service provided by employees, so inadequate service from employees is a major source of service quality problems.

b. It is essential to provide satisfactory service quality to service employees as well.

③ Viewing Customers as Numbers

Overlooking the importance of individual customers can increase dissatisfaction and ultimately lead to service quality issues.

④ Communication Differences

This includes not only exaggerated advertising by the company but also failure to accurately convey the services provided to customers and not listening carefully to customer demands.

⑤ Company's Short-Term Perspective

Emphasizing short-term profits and focusing on cost reduction without prioritizing customer interests ultimately degrades service quality.

(2) Methods for Improving Service Quality

① Identifying Key Determinants of Service Quality: Improving service quality starts with identifying the key determinants of service quality that are important to customers.

② Managing Customer Expectations: Customer expectations play a crucial role in their perception of quality. Providing appropriate service information and avoiding over-promises help achieve a positive quality image for the company.

③ Managing Tangible Elements: Managing tangible elements relates to evaluations during or after service delivery. Customers can easily access and evaluate these tangible elements, so their management influences the assessment of service quality.

④ Providing Service Information to Customers: Enhancing customer knowledge by allowing them to perform parts of the service themselves, or by explaining the appropriate timing, methods, or processes of the service, can improve decision-making and increase customer satisfaction.

⑤ Establishing a Quality Culture within the Company: To maintain consistently high service quality, the concept of quality must be embedded within the company culture. This involves setting specific quality standards, hiring employees capable of meeting these standards, training them to achieve these standards, and measuring satisfaction to ensure fair compensation.

⑥ Implementing Automation: In service delivery, automation systems can reduce errors by replacing areas of human activity that are technically automatable with automated systems.

⑦ Responding to Changing Customer Expectations: Customer expectations change in two ways: the 'level' of expectations increases and the 'perspective' changes. Service companies need to anticipate and address these changes in customer expectations.

⑧ Enhancing Company Image: To become a provider of high-quality services, a company's credibility and image are essential.

⑨ Providing Visible Evaluation Criteria: It is crucial for companies to provide customers with visible evaluation criteria.

7.4 Service Quality and Employees

(1) Conceptual Changes in Marketing Management

Marketing activities should be carried out in a manner that is efficient, effective, and socially responsible. Organizations can use four marketing concepts to guide their marketing activities: 1) Production Concept, 2) Product Concept, 3) Sales Concept, and 4) Marketing Concept.

① Production Concept

This concept assumes that consumers will prefer inexpensive products that are readily available in the market. It is represented by Ford's approach, which aimed to achieve economies of scale through mass production and price reductions to enhance consumer welfare.

② Product Concept

This concept believes that consumers will prefer products that offer the highest quality, performance, and innovative features.

③ Sales Concept

According to this concept, if organizations simply leave customers alone, they will not purchase enough products on their own. Therefore, aggressive sales and promotional efforts are necessary. This concept is often dominant when there is an oversupply of products.

④ Marketing Concept

To achieve organizational goals, this philosophy focuses on creating, delivering, and communicating superior customer value to the selected target market, rather than being product-centric. It is a customer-centric approach that emphasizes treating customers with care and attention, parallel to nurturing a garden rather than merely hunting for sales. In this philosophy, understanding customer needs is crucial for enhancing organizational performance, and customer orientation is considered essential not only for businesses but also for non-profit organizations such as universities, hospitals, museums, and symphonies. This approach is also rapidly spreading in countries like China, which are quickly adopting market economy principles to boost national competitiveness.

(2) Service Marketing Triangle

Service marketing requires not only 'external marketing', which refers to marketing similar to that in manufacturing industries, but also 'interaction marketing' between employees and customers who directly interact while providing services. Additionally, it involves 'internal marketing', which supports and trains employees to deliver the best possible service to customers.

① Internal Marketing

Recently, the role of internal marketing has grown as it focuses on hiring, training, and motivating employees to deliver high levels of service to customers. Internal marketing involves integrating various marketing functions such as sales, advertising, customer service, product management, and marketing research. Furthermore, marketing should be embraced by other departments. It is not just the responsibility of one department but involves all departments, considering how their activities impact the customer.

a. Marketing between the company and employees

b. Marketing activities targeting internal employees to train, motivate, and manage service quality

c. Internal marketing should be prioritized over external marketing

d. The company's CEO should grant employees appropriate levels of discretion, enabling them to identify customer needs, respond swiftly to customer dissatisfaction, and interact with customers with a sense of ownership and responsibility.

② External Marketing

a. Marketing conducted between the company and customers

b. In the service industry, the CEO is responsible for researching customers, designing and planning the services to be provided, and promising the quality of the services offered.

③ Interaction Marketing

a. Marketing conducted between employees and customers (customer contact marketing)

b. Employees of service companies interact directly with customers while providing actual services (delivering on promises, providing services).

(3) Role Conflict and Role Ambiguity of Service Employees

① Employee Role Conflict

a. Role conflict occurs when an individual is given two or more expectations that cannot be simultaneously fulfilled.

b. Employees who interact with customers must connect the company and the customers, satisfying the demands of both simultaneously, leading to role conflict in their duties. Eliminating such role conflicts is essential to satisfying employees.

② Employee Role Ambiguity

a. Role ambiguity occurs when an individual lacks sufficient information related to their role.

- When expectations for performance are unclear
- When unsure how to meet expectations
- When unaware of the outcomes of job behaviors

b. Causes

- When there are no service standards
- When there are too many service standards with conflicting priorities
- When service standards are not communicated properly
- When service standards are not linked to performance measurement, evaluation, and reward system

(4) Employee Satisfaction and Customer Satisfaction

① To achieve success in internal marketing, it is essential to first recognize the role and importance of employees.

② Employee Satisfaction (ES) leads to high-quality service, which directly translates to Customer Satisfaction (CS).

③ Customer Satisfaction leads to customer retention and increased profits. Therefore, the increase in profits for service companies can be achieved through customer satisfaction, which results from employee satisfaction.

(5) Strategies for Improving Employee Satisfaction

① Measuring Employee Satisfaction

a. To improve employee satisfaction, it is crucial first to measure the level of employee satisfaction. Employee satisfaction is a key element in a quality-oriented business strategy.

b. Internal customer satisfaction is influenced by economic factors like compensation and internal service quality factors such as management environment and systems, in other words internal marketing factors.

c. Internal marketing should be activated by applying principles and techniques related to motivation, human resource management, and marketing.

Survey Target		CS Management
All Employees		•Degree of Awareness Sharing

	Internal/External Customer Satisfaction Management (arrow pointing to the right) Right Side	•Participation Spirit •Organizational Culture Satisfaction
CS Management		•System Satisfaction •Job Satisfaction •Overall Satisfaction
•Customer Satisfaction through Internal/ External Customer Satisfaction •Management Practices Center		Survey Target
		Seeking ESI Improvement Plans

② Employee Satisfaction Index (ESI) Survey Items

a. Degree of Shared Perception

b. Spirit of Participation

c. Job Satisfaction

d. Satisfaction with Systems

e. Satisfaction with Organizational Culture

f. Overall Satisfaction

(6) Integrated Human Resource Management

To provide management and service quality that satisfies external customers, efforts to improve service quality must be based on employee capabilities and voluntary motivation. Additionally, the entire process, from the selection of personnel to evaluation and compensation, should be planned and managed integratively to support these efforts.

① Selection: Hire human resources suited to service characteristics and customer satisfaction.

② Job Design: Consider the characteristics of customers, organizational attributes, personnel, and stakeholders.

③ Strengthen Training and Development Programs: Achieve higher performance efficiency.

④ Recognition and Motivation: Operate monetary and non-monetary reward programs.

⑤ Work Environment and Welfare: Ensure high levels of employee motivation and satisfaction.

⑥ Feedback: Evaluate and improve performance at both organizational and individual levels.

(7) Challenges in Service Human Resource Management

① Empowerment

  a. Employee Empowerment: Provide autonomy in job performance to allow
    employees to fully utilize their personal potential. Empowerment can be
    described as a function of two variables: potential and opportunity.

  b. Organizational Control Systems

   • Trust System: Well-implemented organizational culture.

   • Limitation System: Regulations on the limits of employee discretion.

   • Diagnostic System: Definition of measurable achievement goals.

   • Interaction System: Most suitable for knowledge industries.

| Organizational Control Systems for Employee Empowerment |

Control System	Goals	Employees' Tasks	Managers' Tasks	Key Issues
Trust	Contribution	Uncertainty towards Goals	Communication of Core Values and Mission	Identification of Core Values
Limitations	Compliance	Pressure or Temptation	Definition and Enforcement of Standards	Risk Avoidance
Diagnosis	Achievement	Lack of Focus	Establishment and Support of Clear Targets	Key Performance Variables
Interaction	Creation	Lack of Opportunities or Fear of Risk	Opening Organizational Dialogue to Promote Learning	Strategic Uncertainty

② Team Activities : A team refers to a small group with a common purpose, setting its own performance goals and approach, and being responsible for success.

   a. Problem-Solving Team: A small group composed of managers and workers who identify, analyze, and find solutions to production and quality-related problems.

   b. Special-Purpose Team: Addresses major concerns of management, workers, or both (such as customer service issues). Special-purpose teams usually consist of representatives from multiple departments or functions.

   c. Self-Managed Team: Represents the highest level of worker participation, where a small group of workers jointly produces a significant part or the entirety of a product or service. Members learn all necessary tasks, rotate jobs, and handle management duties including work and vacation schedules, supply procurement, and employment.

③ Organizational Structure

   a. Vertical Structure: Departments such as marketing, production, finance, human resources, and public affairs exist, and members wait for directives and approvals from department heads. They are focused on their departmental roles and communicate little across departmental boundaries.

   b. Horizontal Structure: Hierarchical and functional boundaries are removed, and organizational operations are managed by multifunctional teams.

     • Process-centered structure

     • Flat organizational hierarchy

     • Management of the organization by teams

     • Customer-oriented performance

- Executive rewards based on team performance
- Team interactions with customers
- Training programs for all employees

④ Suggestion System

a. A system aimed at maximizing improvement effects by presenting ideas that are considered beneficial to the company throughout the overall service process.

b. Encourages participation by rewarding members who make suggestions related to service improvement, thereby enhancing their sense of involvement and achieving ultimate improvements through their contributions.

Service Leadership

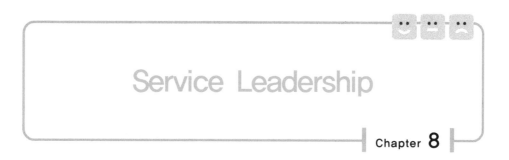

Service Leadership

Chapter **8**

8.1 ╺ Definition of Service Leadership

(1) Definition of Service Leadership

Service leadership is the leadership that is demonstrated through a series of positive cycles, including detecting changes in the environment, identifying opportunities and threats, responding appropriately, securing and utilizing core competencies to achieve public goals, and generating exceptional performance. In other words, it is leadership that ensures a virtuous cycle where internal customer happiness and external customer satisfaction are achieved through the leader's service.

① Leadership is the influence used to set common goals and bring about the cooperation of members to achieve them.

② It is a theory that structures the reality where internal customers (employees) feel satisfaction when they are treated and served as customers by the leader, and based on that satisfaction, provide services that create satisfaction and impressions for external customers.

(2) Types of Service Leadership Theory

The types of service leadership have evolved through interactions among people who wish to lead in ways that form new organizational cultures, transforming from past dominant management logics and creating new values in service leadership. Therefore, leadership reflects the influence (power) that the group exerts to achieve vision and goals, and in organizational behavior, informal leadership is also important.

① Trait Theory

Trait theory, which was primarily used in early leadership research, studies personality, sociability, and physical or intellectual abilities to show the differences between leaders and non-leaders. A limitation of this theory is that it predicts personal traits of leadership rather than differentiating between effective and ineffective leaders. Trait theory is more suited for predicting the emergence of leaders and the appearance of leadership.

② Behavioral Theory

Behavioral theory posits that leaders are developed through training and effort. It involves defining and organizing the roles of subordinates to achieve goals. It includes task-oriented leadership and relationship-oriented leadership, which respects subordinates' ideas based on neutral trust and focuses on motivational support.

③ Contingency Theory

Contingency theory asserts that a leader's behavior must be appropriate to the situation. It involves determining whether to adopt a directive or relational approach based on the circumstances in order to effectively exercise leadership.

a. Contingency Theory – Fiedler's Model[35]

This theory argues that effective group performance occurs when the leader's style and the favorability of the situation align. To determine a leadership style, an evaluation of the Least Preferred Co-worker (LPC) is conducted. If the LPC score is high, it indicates a relationship-oriented leadership style. Conversely, a low LPC score suggests a directive or task-oriented leadership style.

b. Situational Leadership Theory – Paul Hersey & Ken Blanchard[36]

This theory focuses on subordinates and is based on the premise that effective leadership depends on how well the leader meets the needs of the organization's members. It illustrates effective leadership types through the interaction of three elements: the leader's task behaviors, the leader's relationship behaviors, and the maturity level of the organizational members.

---

35) Fiddler, F. E. (1966). *A Review of Research on ASo and LPC Scores as Measures of Leadership Style.*

36) Hersey, P., & Blanchard, K. H. (1982). Principles and Situationalism: Both! A Response to Blake and Mouton. *Group & Organization Studies, 7*(2), 207–210.

c. Path—Goal Theory — Robert House[37]

This theory posits that outstanding leaders clarify the purpose of work for employees and facilitate a comfortable working environment to achieve that purpose. It integrates structured and supportive leadership with motivational expectancy theory. Thus, the leader helps members by presenting desired rewards and clarifying the methods and processes (paths) to achieve goals.

d. The Vroom—Yetton Decision Model — Vroom & Yetton[38]

This theory suggests involving subordinates in the decision-making process but ultimately leaving the final decision to the leader. It incorporates expectancy theory of motivation, indicating that different leadership styles are appropriate depending on the decision-making situation.

④ Leader—Member Exchange Theory (LMX Theory)

This theory is based on a one-on-one exchange relationship between the leader and each subordinate. It classifies employees into in-group and out-group categories based on the level of interaction with the leader. Employees with closer, more personal relationships with the leader (in-group) receive rewards, while those with less personal relationships (out-group) may receive penalties.

⑤ Servant Leadership

A leadership style where the leader's self-sacrifice leads to the voluntary sacrifice of members. It helps members overcome opportunism and anxiety,

---

37) House, R. J. (1971). A Path Goal Theory of Leader Effectiveness. *Administrative Science Quarterly, 16*(3), 321–339.

38) Vroom, V. H., & Yetton, P. W. (1973). *Leadership and Decision-Making*. University of Pittsburgh Press.

stimulates proactive behavior, and enhances the organization's adaptability to environmental changes.

⑥ Transformational Leadership

A leadership style aimed at changing subordinates' beliefs, desires, and values. It transforms subordinates into leaders and leaders into motivators, seeking to achieve mutual stimulation and facilitation of change.

⑦ Emotional Leadership

In contrast to past leadership styles emphasizing reason and logic, this style focuses on forming empathy and social skills. It involves psychologically stimulating members to develop their abilities and effectively achieve organizational goals.

| LMX(Leader Member Exchange) Theory |

The LMX (Leader-Member Exchange) theory[39], which evolved from the VDL (Vertical Dyad Linkage) theory[40], is based on the core assumption that the quality of the relationship between leaders and members affects organizational behavior outcomes. Therefore, LMX theory examines the effects of the relationship between leaders and members as a causal factor of organizational effectiveness, and it develops as the quality of exchanges between leaders and members improves.

The three representative factors for developing engagement between leaders and members are: first, mutual respect between leaders and members is necessary; second, there must be high levels of trust between them; and third, there must be a belief that each other's success and competitiveness can be mutually beneficial.

---

39) Erdogan, B., & Bauer, T. N. (2015). Leader-Member Exchange Theory. In J. D. B. T.-I. E. of the S. & B. S. (Second E. Wright (Ed.), *International Encyclopedia of the Social & Behavioral Sciences* (pp. 641-647). Elsevier.

40) Dansereau, F., Graen, G., & Haga, W. J. (1975). A Vertical Dyad Linkage Approach to Leadership Within Formal Organizations: A Longitudinal Investigation of The Role Making Process. *Organizational Behavior and Human Performance, 13*(1), 46-78.

(3) Classification of Service Leadership

① Leadership can be broadly divided into two aspects.

    a. Internal Aspects of the Organization (Organizational Leadership): Focuses on establishing a well-functioning leadership system within the organization. This includes communicating the organization's values and direction, performance and expectations, customer and stakeholder-centric management, organizational learning, and management innovation.

    b. External Aspects of the Organization: Refers to the organization's social responsibility and perception, expression methods, and support from the local community.

② To achieve effective leadership, it is essential to systematically analyze and measure how leadership performance is related and to establish a feedback system.

(4) Goals of Service Leadership

The goal of service leadership is customer satisfaction. This encompasses both internal customer (service providers) satisfaction and external customer (service buyers) satisfaction. Through service activities, the leader satisfies internal customers who are partners, and these partners, in turn, satisfy external customers who are also partners, creating a cycle of positive reinforcement. Service leadership aims to increase behaviors that lead to partner satisfaction while reducing actions that might undermine satisfaction. To achieve this, service leaders require various approaches and efforts.

8.2 ⟶ Core Elements of Service Leadership

(1) Core Elements of Service Leadership

The core elements of service leadership are Service Concept, Mind, and Skill. When these three elements are in harmony, customer satisfaction can be achieved. This can be expressed with the formula 'C × M × S = Customer Satisfaction'. Only when a service leader possesses all three components 'C, M, and S' in a multiplicative relationship can they truly exhibit desirable leader behaviors, which lead to employee satisfaction and ultimately to customer satisfaction.

(2) 9 Detailed Components of C · M · S

Research on C·M·S has been conducted through field studies and various leadership research. Since C·M·S comprises three sub-elements each, it consists of a total of nine sub-elements. Service leaders should develop and cultivate these 9 elements.

① Service Concept

    a. It can be explained through the philosophy that lays the foundation of service leadership, the vision that everyone wants to share, and the innovation of how we will improve the present for this purpose. Unless the concept of service is organized in the mind and it becomes a belief, service behavior that leads to customer satisfaction will not be possible.

    b. Belief consists of three sub-elements: philosophy, vision, and innovation, and can be compared to the head of the human body.

② Service Mind

    a. This refers to the mindset or attitude of wanting to form partnerships and provide satisfaction. When this mindset is established, the leader's actions naturally lead to customer satisfaction.

    b. It refers to the mind, attitude, and mental stance that a service leader should have, describing a state where the concepts formed in the mind have settled in the heart. As the saying goes, 'You can lead a horse to water, but you can't make it drink', unless the desire arises naturally from within, customer satisfaction-oriented service will not occur.

    c. The domain of attitude consists of three elements: passion, affection, and trust. It refers to the mindset or attitude of wondering, 'How can I get closer to the partner, form a partnership, and solve their difficulties?' It describes a state or attitude of wanting to get closer to the partner to provide love, joy, satisfaction, and create a sense of fulfillment. When this mindset is established, the leader's actions naturally lead to customer satisfaction, and the domain of attitude can be compared to the heart of the human body.

③ Service Skill

    a. This is divided into the ability to identify customers' needs and the ability to satisfy them. To fulfill the identified needs, one must possess the ability to create services, manage and operate efficiently, and form and improve human relationships. Satisfying the needs of partners requires the continuous creation of new service methods and the ability to maintain the current state of service. Without maintaining the current state, it is impossible to progress to the next stage. Therefore, the ability to develop these services in an organized and systematic manner through human relationship skills is essential.

b. Since service is an issue that arises between humans, not machines, it cannot be properly delivered without human relationship skills. If service ability were compared to the human body, it would correspond to the hands and feet. Thus, the domain of service ability is summarized into three elements: creative ability, operational ability, and relational ability.

8.3 Role of a Service Leader

(1) Importance of Leadership

A service leader will only exhibit desirable leadership behavior when they equally possess the three elements of C, M, and S, which together form a multiplicative relationship. This leadership behavior leads to partner satisfaction and ultimately to the satisfaction of external customers.

The multiplicative relationship fundamentally differs from an additive one. In an additive relationship, if any one or two elements are high, the total sum can still be high regardless of the other elements. However, in a multiplicative relationship, if any element is negative or zero, the total becomes negative or zero.

(2) Curt Reimann's Characteristics of Excellent Leadership[41]

① Accessibility to Customers: A leader demonstrates leadership with the customer in mind.

② Combination of Leading by Example and Accurate Knowledge: A leader knows exactly what to do and how to do it and leads by example.

③ Passion for Work: A leader possesses more passion for their work than anyone else.

④ Challenging Goals: A leader sets challenging goals that are somewhat difficult to achieve.

⑤ Strong Drive: A leader has the capability to strongly push forward with tasks.

⑥ Cultural Change within the Company: A leader informs employees about the values the company pursues and ultimately transforms the corporate culture in the desired direction.

⑦ Organization: A leader systematically organizes and implements all of the above elements effectively.

(3) Service Leader's Role Performance

① Understanding Oneself

A leader must first and foremost understand themselves, identifying their strengths and weaknesses. By doing so, they can enhance their strengths and

---

41) Reimann, C. W., & Hertz, H. S. (1996). The Baldrige Award and ISO 9000 Registration Compared. *The Journal for Quality and Participation, 19*(1), 12.

attempt to eliminate their weaknesses, leading to a more developed and effective leadership style.

② Leader and Team Members

a. A leader must make team members recognize that the success of the organization is the result of the collective effort and cooperation of all members, not the outstanding talent of any single individual.

b. A leader should empower team members by delegating authority, enabling them to make decisions that satisfy both the organization and its customers. This empowerment helps team members develop their decision-making skills and allows the leader to demonstrate their leadership capabilities.

c. Customers expect high-quality service from team members with leadership skills, so internal customers (team members) must strive to develop their leadership abilities to meet these expectations.

③ Leader as Counselor or Coach for Team Members

a. A leader should continually train, praise, and encourage team members to ensure they can provide services that impress customers.

b. A leader must always be attentive to and address the work-related difficulties and concerns of team members.

c. As a coach, a leader should delegate authority and responsibility to team members who have mastered their tasks, enabling them to provide services more responsibly.

d. As a counselor, a leader should adopt an open attitude, gathering opinions from various people to foster innovative and creative work performance, which will significantly help team members provide satisfying support to customers.

| Development Process of Leadership Theories |

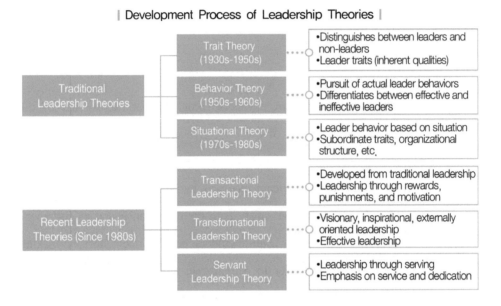

(4) Servant Leadership

① Definition

This theory was first proposed by Robert K. Greenleaf in the late 1970s[42]. It emphasizes the importance of relationship management with subordinates, viewing them as the most critical resources. It involves a leadership style where the leader serves their subordinates diligently, sharing all their experiences and expertise. Therefore, instead of control, the leader exercises their leadership through listening, empathy, praise and encouragement, and persuasion.

---

42) Greenleaf, R. K. (1970). *The Servant as Leader*. Greenleaf Publishing Center.

② 10 Characteristics of Servant Leadership

a. Attitude of Listening

Listening includes hearing the inner voices that are not outwardly expressed. Paired with moments of reflection, listening is essential for the proper growth of a servant leader.

b. Attitude of Empathy

Servant leaders strive to understand and empathize with their employees. Each person's unique and special characteristics should be recognized. Servant leaders approach people with an attitude of acknowledging and empathizing with their individuality.

c. Interest in Healing

Many employees are discouraged and suffer from various emotional wounds. One of the most powerful impacts a servant leader can have is showing concern for healing these wounds and pains.

d. Clear Awareness

Servant leaders differ from "servants" in that they do not serve unconditionally. They provide reasonable alternatives based on a clear understanding of the situation. The decisions and attitudes of a servant leader are rooted in this clear awareness.

e. Persuasion

Another characteristic of servant leaders is their reliance on persuasion rather than authority. They convince others rather than force obedience distinguishing them from traditional authoritarian models.

f. Broad Thinking

Traditional leaders often exhaust their energy achieving short-term goals.

In contrast, servant leaders think more broadly, aiming to take appropriate actions in the present with a vision for the future.

g. Insight

Servant leaders use insight to help employees understand lessons from the past. This understanding leads to a clear perception of reality and enables the prediction of future outcomes based on decisions made.

h. Responsibility

Servant leaders view their roles as positions of service to others. Their primary focus is dedication to others.

i. Commitment to the Growth of People

Believing in the intrinsic value of people beyond their work contributions, servant leaders engage in concrete actions such as securing funds for their development, showing interest in ideas and suggestions from all members, encouraging employee involvement in decision-making, and actively helping laid-off employees find new jobs.

j. Building Community

Servant leaders strive to create a sense of community within the organization, believing that a genuine community can be formed among those working together.

| Traditional Leader vs. Servant Leader |

Category	Traditional Leader	Servant Leader
Focus Area	Results of work	Obstacles in work progress
Values	Self-centered, directives and supervision based on personal standards	Open, trusting and accepting of people, positive, humorous

View of People	Objects to be directed to achieve results	People to be helped, targets of success and growth
Task and People Importance	Task first	People first
Hierarchy	Command and obedience	Respect and concern
Work Approach	Emphasizes own method	Seeks ideas
Productivity	Emphasizes quantitative measures like time, cost, and output	Emphasizes voluntary actions of team members
Sense of Time	Always lacks time	Makes time for themselves
View on Competition	Encourages internal competition, devises competitive mechanisms	Avoids excessive competition, emphasizes belief that everyone can excel
Evaluation	Result-oriented	Effort-oriented

(5) Participative Service Leadership

① Definition

Participative service leadership is a form of leadership that actively involves organizational members in the organizational processes, incorporating their opinions into decision-making. This approach aims to motivate individuals and internalize organizational goals within themselves, which, in turn, enhances their performance.

② Characteristics of Participative Service Leadership

a. Elicits and reflects the thoughts, information, and preferences of subordinates in major administrative decisions.

b. Delegates decision-making authority to subordinates in areas where they are accountable.

c. Grants front-line employees the authority to choose methods of executing decisions made by higher-ups.

d. Senior managers do not relinquish their authority and responsibility; they retain ultimate authority to nullify or amend subordinates' decisions when necessary.

③ Advantages and Disadvantages of Participative Service Leadership

Advantages	Disadvantages
① Increased motivation for participating in organizational goals	① Time-consuming
② Easier utilization of group knowledge and skills	② Reaching mediocre decisions due to compromises
③ Enhanced commitment to organizational activities	③ Powerlessness due to diffusion of responsibility
④ Promotion of personal values and beliefs	④ Difficulty in finding dedicated and visionary leaders
⑤ Learning management thinking and skills through participation	⑤ Challenging to learn participative style
⑥ Encouragement of free communication	⑥ Limited effectiveness when team members have similar values

(6) Emotional Service Leadership

① Definition

a. Emotional Intelligence (EQ): This refers to the ability to objectively assess one's limitations and potential, manage one's emotions well, truly understand others from their perspective, and maintain good relationships with others.

b. Emotional Leadership: This type of leadership focuses on the emotions of organizational members, forming emotional connections and systematizing this process so that members can fully utilize their abilities to achieve the organization's goals. Daniel Goleman, who first introduced the concept of emotional intelligence, described great leaders in his book Emotional

Leadership as those who can tune into their own and others' emotional frequencies. According to Goleman, what makes a true leader is 'emotion', and when a leader draws 'empathy' rather than mere 'response' from members, they can achieve their goals and their followers can experience transformation.

c. Successful and Unsuccessful Leaders: Daniel Goleman's research concluded that the difference between successful and unsuccessful leaders is largely influenced by emotional intelligence rather than technical skills or IQ. He found that approximately 80% emotional intelligence and 20% cognitive abilities create the right balance for leaders to effectively exercise leadership.

② Four Elements of Emotional Competence

Emotional competence refers to the ability to align and manage one's emotional code with that of the team members, and it consists of the following four elements:

a. Self-awareness: This refers to the degree to which one can clearly and objectively understand and positively affirm one's values, emotional states, strengths and weaknesses, and goals. In other words, it means having a good understanding of oneself.

b. Self-management: This is the ability to appropriately control and manage one's emotions. To be an emotional leader, it is essential not only to understand oneself but also to be able to manage oneself. Particularly, it involves controlling negative emotions (such as anger and dissatisfaction) that can cause anxiety among team members and maintaining an optimistic and joyful attitude.

c. Social-awareness: This is the ability to deeply understand the emotions and states of team members, also known as the ability to show affection and consideration for others. This competence requires the leader to listen to and understand the situations of team members first, and then effectively communicate the leader's perspective to them.

d. Challenge Spirit and Passion: The source of emotional leadership lies in a high level of challenge spirit and passion. When a leader demonstrates relentless passion and perseverance toward challenging goals, team members will, in turn, develop loyalty and follow the leader with trust.

③ Five Elements of Emotional Intelligence

a. Self-awareness: The ability to recognize and understand one's own emotions, moods, and preferences, and how they affect others. This includes self-awareness, self-assessment, and self-confidence.

b. Self-regulation: The ability to control or redirect negative moods and behaviors. This includes self-control, trustworthiness, conscientiousness, adaptability, and innovativeness.

c. Motivation: The ability to pursue goals with energy and persistence, driven by internal rewards such as personal interest and enjoyment rather than external rewards like money or fame. This includes drive, commitment, initiative, and optimism.

d. Empathy: The ability to understand and share the feelings of others. This includes understanding others, empathizing with subordinates, and having strategic awareness.

e. Social Skills (Interpersonal Skills): The ability to build and manage relationships effectively, and to respond appropriately to the emotions of others. This includes influencing others, communication, conflict management, leadership, transformational abilities, relationship building, cooperation, and team-building skills.

8.4 ✦ Motivation Theory

Motivation is the act of stimulating or inspiring someone to take action, consisting of three elements:

1) Direction: The purpose or goal towards which behavior is oriented.

2) Persistence: The sustained effort and continuous behavior until the goal is achieved.

3) Intensity: The strength or enthusiasm of the behavior, often referred to as passion.

Motivation theories related to organizational situations are categorized into content theories, process theories, and reinforcement theories.

Content Theories: Focus on identifying the needs that drive individual behavior (the content and fulfillment of needs). They aim to understand what motivates individuals to act and are known as need theories. These theories suggest that unmet needs trigger motivation.

Process Theories: Focus on the motivational processes and mechanisms that lead to motivated behavior. They explain how motivation occurs through various stages or processes.

Reinforcement Theories: Address why the motivation process occurs. They suggest that behavior is determined by its environmental consequences, known as the Law of Effect. These theories propose that behaviors followed by positive outcomes are likely to be repeated, while behaviors followed by negative outcomes are less likely to be repeated.

| Content Theory vs. Process Theory vs. Reinforcement Theory |

Content Theory	Process Theory	Reinforcement Theory
Maslow's Hierarchy of Needs Theory	Vroom's Expectancy Theory	Skinner's Reinforcement Theory
Herzberg's Two-Factor Theory	Adams' Equity Theory	
McGregor's Theory X and Theory Y	Locke's Goal-Setting Theory	
Alderfer's ERG Theory	Deci's Cognitive Evaluation Theory	

(1) Content Theories of Motivation

Content theories of motivation are concerned with identifying people's needs, their relative intensities, and the goals people pursue to satisfy these needs.

① Maslow's Hierarchy of Needs Theory[43]

Maslow's Hierarchy of Needs Theory, published in 1943, originates from his theory on personal development and motivation. He proposed that there are two types of needs that drive human behavior: deficiency needs and growth needs. The fundamental premise is that humans are inherently deficient beings, constantly seeking more, and their actions are determined by what they want and what they already have.

Maslow suggested that human needs are arranged in a hierarchy of importance, with needs at each level motivating behavior. Once the lowest-level needs

---

43) Maslow, A. H. (1943). A Theory of Human Motivation. *Psychological Review, 50*(4), 370–396.

are satisfied, they no longer serve as strong motivators, and the individual moves on to fulfill higher-level needs. According to this theory, behavior is initially driven by the desire to satisfy the most basic needs, and as each need is met, the individual progresses to the next level of needs.

In Maslow's Hierarchy of Needs theory, the next higher-level need in the hierarchy becomes the most powerful motivator once lower-level needs are satisfied. While the order of needs in the hierarchy generally holds true, there can be exceptions, and for some individuals, the hierarchy may be reversed.

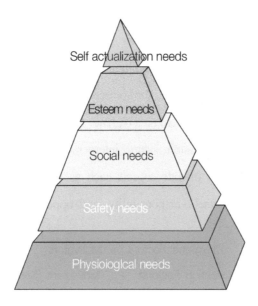

(2) Herzberg's Two-Factor Theory[44]

Herzberg's Two-Factor Theory was developed based on interviews with accountants and engineers from 11 companies in Pittsburgh, USA. Using recall methods to measure human attitudes, Herzberg discovered that factors

---

44) Herzberg, F. (1964). The Motivation-Hygiene Concept and Problems of Manpower. *Personnel Administration, 27*(1), 3-7.

influencing job preferences differed and categorized them into two sets: hygiene factors (dissatisfaction factors) and motivators (satisfaction factors). This theory explains motivation by focusing on these two types of factors. Hygiene factors, if absent, cause dissatisfaction, while motivators encourage individuals to put in greater effort and perform better. Hygiene factors are roughly related to the lower-level needs in Maslow's hierarchy, and motivators are related to the higher-level needs. Therefore, addressing hygiene factors can prevent dissatisfaction but does not, by itself, create positive attitudes or motivation. Motivators, on the other hand, are the factors that truly drive people to perform and excel in their work.

Herzberg's Two-Factor Theory explains that the absence of hygiene factors leads to dissatisfaction, while the presence of motivators leads to higher motivation and job satisfaction. Hygiene factors include aspects such as company policies, supervision, salary, interpersonal relationships, and working conditions. Motivators include aspects such as achievement, recognition, the nature of the work itself, responsibility, and opportunities for advancement.

| Hygiene Factors vs. Motivators |

Hygiene Factors (Dissatisfaction Factors)	Motivators (Satisfaction Factors)
Company policies and administration	Achievement
Supervision (technical)	Recognition
Salary	The work itself

(3) McGregor's Theory X and Theory Y[45]

McGregor's Theory X and Theory Y investigates managers' perceptions of employees. Through his research, McGregor discovered that managers' views of human nature can be split into two categories: those with a negative outlook and those with a positive outlook. The negative view is categorized as Theory X, which suggests that to achieve organizational goals, there must be control through threats such as punishment. The positive view is categorized as Theory Y, which suggests that motivating employees to achieve goals is best accomplished through rewards and recognition, allowing for autonomy.

(4) Alderfer's ERG Theory[46]

Alderfer's ERG Theory simplifies Maslow's five stages of needs into three categories: Existence, Relatedness, and Growth. Existence needs refer to the basic survival needs, which encompass Maslow's physiological and safety needs. Relatedness needs involve the desire for social relationships, love, belonging, and interpersonal connections, aligning with Maslow's social needs. Growth needs pertain to personal development and self-esteem, focusing on the desire to grow, develop, and realize one's potential, similar to Maslow's esteem needs.

(5) McClelland's Achievement Motivation Theory[47]

McClelland's Achievement Motivation Theory focuses on the higher-level needs identified by Maslow, categorizing them into three types: the need for

---

45) McGregor, D. (1960). *The Human Side of Enterprise.* McGraw-Hill.

46) Alderfer, C. P. (1969). An Empirical Test of a New Theory of Human Needs. *Organizational Behavior and Human Performance, 4*(2), 142–175.

47) McClelland, D. C. (1965). Toward a Theory of Motive Acquisition. *American Psychologist, 20*(5), 321–333.

achievement, the need for affiliation, and the need for power. The relative intensity of these three needs varies from person to person.

Need for Achievement	Need for Belongings	Need for Power
The desire to accomplish something significant	The desire to get along well with others	The desire to influence others
The desire to solve problems independently	The desire for frequent interpersonal relationships	The desire to be in a leadership position
The desire to achieve goals, even if it involves taking risks	The desire for group-oriented tasks	The desire to persuade others or take the lead
The desire to outperform others	The desire for communication opportunities	The desire to take responsibility and show interest in improving one's status

(2) Motivation Process Theories

① Vroom's Expectancy Theory[48]

Vroom's Expectancy Theory posits that individuals are motivated by the attractiveness and utility of the outcomes that may result from their actions, based on economic rationality. Motivation arises from the combination of Expectancy, Instrumentality, and Valence. The level of motivation is determined by the anticipated results of these elements.

② Adams' Equity Theory[49]

Adams' Equity Theory explains how individuals strive to achieve Fairness or Justice in social exchange relationships. It focuses on personal perceptions of how fairly one is being treated in comparison to others.

---

48) Vroom, V. H. (1964). Work and Motivation. In *Work and motivation*. Wiley.

49) Adams, J. S. (1963). Towards an Understanding of Inequity. In *The Journal of Abnormal and Social Psychology* (Vol. 67, Issue 5, pp. 422-436). American Psychological Association.

③ Locke's Goal-Setting Theory[50]

Locke's Goal-Setting Theory is the foundation for the Management By Objectives (MBO) technique. This theory explains that setting specific and challenging goals leads to motivation. The behavior of organizational members is influenced more by goals and values than by mere desires. Clear and challenging goals lead to higher performance and motivation levels among members.

(3) Motivation Reinforcement Theory

Skinner's reinforcement theory is based on the Law of Effect, which suggests that behaviors are repeated when they result in positive outcomes, and it aims to solidify the thoughts, attitudes, and knowledge of the learner. This theory uses positive reinforcement (rewards, incentives, vacations, etc.), negative reinforcement, extinction, and punishment (salary cuts, prohibition of assigning other tasks, etc.) to shape behavior through environmental consequences.

8.5 New Service Marketing Approach

(1) Definition of Experiential Marketing

Experiential marketing was first defined in the book Experience Economy by Pine and Gilmore (1998)[51], who are co-founders of the management consulting

---

50) Locke, E. A., & Latham, G. P. (1990). *A Theory of Goal Setting & Task Performance.* (pp. xviii, 413–xviii, 413). Prentice-Hall, Inc.

51) Gilmore, J. H., & Pine, J. (1998). Welcome to the Experience Economy. In *Harvard Business Review.* Harvard Business Press.

firm Strategic Horizons LLP. It is a marketing technique that involves promoting products by allowing customers to directly experience them. Unlike traditional marketing, which focuses on the product's features or benefits, experiential marketing emphasizes creating experiences that stimulate customers' senses through atmosphere, image, or brand. This 21st-century marketing strategy focuses on generating memorable experiences and emotional engagement, making customers more attracted to services that provide unforgettable sensory experiences rather than mere promotional information.

| Four Key Characteristics of Traditional Marketing and Experiential Marketing |

Traditional Marketing	Experiential Marketing
① Emphasizes functional characteristics and benefits ② Ideal consumer engages in consumption ③ Consumes the product ④ Uses analytical, quantitative, and language-centered marketing tools and methods	① Emphasizes customer experience ② Consumer driven by both rational and emotional nature ③ Consumption as a holistic experience ④ Uses diverse marketing tools and methods

(2) Types of Experiential Marketing

① Sensory Marketing

Marketing aimed at providing sensory experiences by stimulating the five senses—sight, hearing, smell, touch, and taste—to create sensory experiences for customers. This requires an understanding of methods that influence sensory organs and includes aesthetic marketing through design, color marketing, scent marketing, and sound marketing.

② Emotional Marketing

a. Appeals to people's feelings and emotions to create emotional experiences, ranging from somewhat positive feelings related to the brand to strong emotions such as joy and pride. However, since most emotions occur during consumption and emotional advertising often does not target the feelings experienced during the consumption process, it is often inadequate. b. To effectively implement emotional marketing, one must understand how specific stimuli can evoke particular emotions and also encourage consumer participation in emotional acceptance and empathy.

③ Cognitive Marketing (Intellectual Marketing)

   a. Aims to provide customers with creative cognitive and problem-solving experiences, appealing to the intellect with 'cognitive experiences'. This is achieved by stimulating surprise, curiosity, and interest to encourage convergent or confirmatory thinking.

   b. Cognitive campaigns are commonly used with high-tech products. However, cognitive marketing is not limited to high-tech products and is also applied in product design across various industries, retail, and communication fields.

④ Behavioral Marketing

   a. Focuses on influencing customers' physical experiences, lifestyles, and interactions.

   b. Enhances customers' physical experiences and enriches their lives by showcasing various methods, lifestyles, and interactions.

   c. Can be influenced by role models such as movie stars or famous athletes.

⑤ Relationship Marketing

   a. Enhances personal experiences through 'relational experiences' that involve forming connections with others, thereby stimulating the customer's desire for self-improvement by linking them to an ideal self, others, or culture.

b. Relates to personal desires for self-development and the need to be positively perceived by others. It also connects individuals to broader social systems, forming strong brand relationships and brand communities.

| Strategic Foundations of Experiential Marketing |

Sensory Marketing	• Integrate sensory elements (key attributes, style, theme, etc.) as part of the sensory strategy (cognitive consistency/sensory diversity) to appeal to customers' aesthetics and excitement. • 4P: assets, products, appearance, publications. • Color: style, theme, overall impression.
Emotional Marketing	• Use emotional stimuli (events, actors, objects) at the point of consumption or in communication as part of the emotional strategy to influence people's moods and feelings.
Cognitive Marketing	• Employ a cognitive approach that is directional, associative, and cognitive, combining surprise, curiosity, and stimulation to appeal to consumers' creative thinking. • Surprise and curiosity through visual, verbal, and conceptual stimuli.
Behavioral Marketing	• Enhance physical experiences and present alternative behaviors and lifestyle patterns, while using experiential marketing to boost social interactions. • Behavioral experiences: physical activities, interactions, lifestyle, non-verbal behaviors, self-perception, behavioral change, rational behavior.
Relationship Marketing	• Connect consumers' personal selves to broader social and cultural contexts reflected in the brand, creating an identity for the customer. • Relational experiences: social influence, social roles, kinship, cultural values, group affiliation, brand community, social identity, social categorization.

Chapter

9

Customer Satisfaction Management

Customer Satisfaction Management

Chapter **9**

9.1 Concept of Customer Satisfaction Management

Customer satisfaction management refers to the practice of providing products or services to customers and meeting their expectations to ensure continued preference for those products or services. In the modern era of mass production, where supply exceeds demand, the importance of customer satisfaction management has grown significantly. In fact, considering that the cost of acquiring new customers is 4 to 5 times higher than retaining existing ones, managing customer satisfaction is directly linked to a company's survival.

9.2 ⋅ History of Customer Satisfaction Management

(1) Indifference Stage (Before 1990s)

① This period was characterized by a focus on company-centric management practices, with the concept of customer satisfaction not yet being introduced.

② In the 1970s, as consumerism matured in the United States, the concept of customer satisfaction management began to gain prominence.

③ In 1977, JD Power, an American research company, set a precedent by publishing rankings of automotive companies based on customer satisfaction, marking the beginning of customer satisfaction as a business evaluation criterion.

④ In 1981, Jan Carlson of the globally recognized Scandinavian Airlines introduced the concept of "Moments of Truth" (MOT), which emphasized critical customer interactions and widely influenced global customer service practices.

⑤ In the late 1980s, amid economic challenges in Japan due to the sharp rise in the yen, Toyota adopted customer satisfaction management as a strategy to address the economic crisis, highlighting the growing importance of customer-centric management approaches.

(2) Introduction and Decline Stage of Customer Satisfaction (1990s to Before 2000)

① Customer-centric management phase. This period saw the introduction of customer satisfaction management, which experienced ups and downs.

② Introduction in South Korea. Since LG first introduced it in 1992, companies such as Samsung in 1993, KT in the mid-1990s, and the Korea National Railroad also followed suit.

③ Recession Due to IMF. In late 1997, the IMF crisis led to a setback in customer satisfaction management.

(3) 2000s Full Introduction of Customer Satisfaction (2000 and Later)

① This marks the stage of customer delight management.

② From the 2000s onwards, customer satisfaction management has been implemented in most companies, regardless of industry.

9.3 ⸱⸱ Service Process Structure

(1) Definition

① From the company's perspective, it represents the process of transforming inputs—such as raw materials, information, and people—into outputs, including services and other results.

② From the customer's perspective, it refers to the collection of all related activities that create value or produce results for the customer.

③ Processes should ultimately enhance business performance.

④ Discipline within a process should focus on improving creativity and efficiency, rather than merely controlling.

⑤ Ultimately, from a teleological perspective, a process allows a company to achieve its goals when all business activities are conducted with the aim of satisfying customers.

(2) Business Processes

① Michael Hammer's Business Process

Michael Hammer defined a business process as "a collection of all related activities that create results for the customer or create value for the customer".

② Business Process

a. Core processes are those that create the final products and services delivered to external customers, crossing the boundaries of the organization's functions.

b. Support processes occur within the organization but affect the performance of core processes.

③ Classification of Business Processes by Edwards & Peppard[52]

Not all processes within an organization contribute equally to the execution of the company's business strategy. Ultimately, an organization should select and focus on processes that are most effective in generating performance. The re-engineering of processes should also be focused on these high-impact areas. To this end, Edwards & Peppard from the UK classified business processes as follows:

---

52) Edwards, C., & Peppard, J. (1997). Operationalizing Strategy through Process. *Long Range Planning, 30*(5), 753-767.

Competing Processes	• Competing processes are those that provide superior customer value compared to competitors. • They focus on satisfying customer needs, and thus can be judged against customer expectations. • For example, if the value demanded by customers is product diversity to suit individual preferences, the company's competing process is a customization process. On the other hand, if competition is based on price, the organization's competing process is one that produces at a lower cost than competit
Transformational Processes	• These are processes aimed at ensuring the organization's continued competitive advantage in rapidly changing environments by combining people, technology, and processes to build future competitiveness. • Examples include new product development and processes for establishing learning organizations to acquire new knowledge.
Foundation Processes	• These are not core processes but are considered valuable to customers based on the process outcomes. • They provide the minimum necessary value to customers, regardless of competition with other organizations. • For example, initially, product quality may have been a major competitive factor, but as quality becomes standardized and design, price, etc., become the main competitive factors, quality is classified as a foundation process.
Support Programs	• These are processes that support the proper execution of the three main processes mentioned above. • They do not directly deliver value to customers and are often regarded as traditional functional activities rather than processes. • Examples include human resource management, financial accounting, and training and development.

④ Usefulness of Process Classification

a. By classifying processes within a company, operational efficiency can be enhanced through the allocation of resources based on the importance of each business process.

b. The classification of business processes focuses reengineering efforts. It prioritizes the competing processes that currently provide a competitive advantage and further directs the organization's capabilities towards transformational processes that secure future competitiveness. Additionally, business process classification serves as a starting point for continuous process innovation, guiding performance improvement efforts such as outsourcing processes that are neither competing nor transformational.

⑤ Standardization and Customization of Service Processes

a. Standardization

Southwest Airlines in the United States successfully implemented a standardization strategy through several measures: operating a point-to-point system rather than a hub-and-spoke model, using smaller airports, offering low fares for short-haul flights, eliminating beverage and meal services, and removing assigned seating.

b. Customization

Singapore Airlines applied a customization strategy successfully by providing services tailored to customer preferences, empowering employees, and offering high-quality services at a relatively higher price.

(3) Classification of Service Processes

① Definition

Service processes can be classified into four categories based on labor intensity, customer interaction, and customization, which is known as the Service Process Matrix.

a. Labor intensity refers to the relative ratio of dependence on capital, such as equipment and facilities needed for service delivery, versus dependence on labor, or the degree of reliance on people.

b. Customer interaction refers to the extent to which customers interact with the service process.

c. Customization refers to the degree to which the service is customized by the customer.

② Classification of the Service Process Matrix

Classification		Customer Interaction / Customization	
		High	Low
Labor Intensity	High	Professional Services (e.g., lawyers, doctors, consultants, architects)	Mass Services (e.g., retail banking, schools, wholesale trade)
	Low	Service Shops (e.g., hospitals, repair centers, other maintenance companies)	Service Factories (e.g., airlines, transportation, hotels, resorts)

(4) Service Process Flow

① Process Flow

A process can be summarized as "the total of value-added activities that use one or more inputs to create an output valuable to the customer". Accordingly, the flow can be represented as follows.

Input	People, equipment, materials, methods, environment, etc.
Process	Value-added activities
Output	Output valuable to the customer (product or service)

② Basic Principles of Process Design

a. The customer is the primary evaluator.

b. Evaluation is relative, not absolute.

c. Evaluation is based on performance compared to expectations.

d. Managing customer expectations is essential.

e. Adapting to the individual needs of customers is important.

f. The most efficient way to adapt to individual customer needs is through frontline employees or support systems.

g. All decisions should consider the customer.

③ The Role of the Customer in the Service Process

a. Temporary Staff: When customers participate in the production and delivery of services, they play a role similar to temporary staff. However, since they cannot be managed like regular employees, this introduces issues of uncertainty.

b. Human Resources: Assigning roles to customers in the service process encourages them to take an active part in their production role. Consequently, they emerge as contributors to productivity, quality, value, and satisfaction.

c. Source of Capability: With advancements in information technology, customers acquire information nearly equivalent to that of companies. Thus, companies need to restructure their service processes to align with this.

d. Innovator: As customers become prominent in the development of new products and services, they also take on the role of innovators for service companies.

④ Managing Dissatisfied Customers

a. Significance

Since it is impossible to provide a service that satisfies 100% of customers, it is crucial to appropriately address dissatisfied customers that arise during the service delivery process and convert them into loyal customers.

b. Reasons for Customer Dissatisfaction

Dissatisfaction may arise even when the service itself is excellent but does not match the unique preferences of individual customers. However, the main causes are often incorrect inputs, improper processes, incorrect instructions, inaccurate execution, and employee mistakes.

c. Methods for Handling Dissatisfied Customers

Companies should always establish proper manuals for identifying the causes and removal methods of customer dissatisfaction through continuous customer monitoring. It is important to proactively understand customer needs and accurately identify the gaps between customer needs and service delivery to design and implement optimal processes.

(5) Management According to the Service Purchase Process

① Pre-Purchase Process - Queue Management

a. Significance

The time customers spend waiting to make a purchase is often a negative experience. Effectively managing wait times is crucial as it enhances customer satisfaction and can lead to repeat purchases. To manage waiting effectively, it is important to understand the following eight principles:

- Time feels longer when doing nothing.
- Pre-purchase waits feel longer.
- Anxiety makes the wait seem longer.
- Waiting without knowing when the service will be received feels longer.

- Waiting without knowing the reason feels longer.
- Unfair waits feel longer.
- The less valuable the wait, the longer it feels.
- Waiting alone feels longer.

b. Queue Management Methods

Queue management can be broadly divided into two methods: production management methods, which involve changing the company's service methods to reduce actual customer wait times, and customer perception management methods, which aim to reduce the perceived wait time experienced by customers without changing the service methods.

Production Management Methods	• Utilization of Reservations: Used in hospitals, family restaurants, airlines, etc. • Utilization of Communication: Providing information about busy/slow times, sending email updates about the process. • Establishing a Fair Waiting System: Using fair queues, number tickets, express lines. • Offering Alternatives: Guiding walk-in customers to online registration and usage, using ARS (Automated Response System), ATMs, automatic transfers, phone, and internet services.
Customer Perception Management Methods	• Creating a Sense of Service Being Provided: Use guides to provide information, facilitate reception, and offer consultations. • Providing Estimated Wait Times: Informing customers of the expected wait time rather than having them wait without any information can reduce perceived wait time. • Tailoring Responses to Customer Types: Handle different customer needs at specific service points, such as directing simple transactions to ATMs, consultations to service counters, and VIP customers to VIP rooms. • Concealing Unused Resources: Perform non-interactive activities out of customers' sight and keep idle employees and unused facilities hidden from view.

② Purchase Process - MOT (Moment of Truth)

a. MOT (Moment of Truth): The moment of truth can be defined as the moment when a customer comes into contact with an employee or specific resource of the company, influencing their perception of the service quality.

b. Jan Carlson, President of Scandinavian Airlines (SAS): He stated that the success or failure of SAS depends on whether they satisfy customers at the moment of truth.

c. Managing the Entire MOT Cycle: The moment of truth is not just a single instance within the entire service but encompasses all direct and indirect moments of interaction with the customer. These moments collectively form the overall evaluation of the service.

d. Multiplication Rule ($97 \times 95 \times 93 \times 91 \times 0 = 0$): Even if each service element scores excellently initially, if the final stage scores zero, the overall result is zero, indicating poor service. This means that every step, from start to finish, must be handled well.

e. Service Providers' Approach: Service providers should not presume they fully understand the customer's needs. Often, the needs of the service provider and the customer differ, so it is crucial to always listen to the customer's demands from their perspective.

③ Post-Purchase Process - Fishbone Diagram

a. Overview

The Fishbone Diagram (also known as the Ishikawa Diagram or Cause-and-Effect Diagram) was developed by Kaoru Ishikawa in Japan. It systematically combines causes and effects using a diagram resembling a fishbone to visualize how various factors interact and influence an outcome.

b. Purpose of the Fishbone Diagram

The diagram aims to identify the root causes of a problem, allowing for improvements in operations in a more desirable direction. It helps determine whether specific elements are causes of the problem or its effects.

c. Example

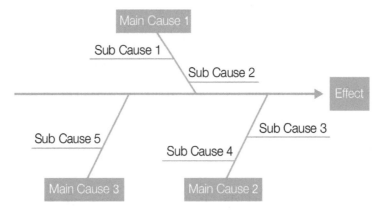

d. Components

It consists of problems and causes. By continuously questioning why these causes occurred, one can identify the root causes and related secondary factors.

Problem (Effect, Characteristic)	To derive the root cause, the problem to be analyzed is described at the head of the fish.
Cause (Main Cause and Sub–Cause)	To identify the causes of the problem, brainstorming is used, paying close attention to distinguish between symptoms and causes. Causes represent the root reasons for the problem and are depicted as diagonal lines in the shape of fishbones on the diagram, with the cause names summarized and noted nearby.

e. Characteristics

The Fishbone Diagram can be seen as a combination of mind mapping, which organizes thoughts radially, and brainwriting, which records only the core of free-flowing ideas.

(6) Methods for Improving Service Processes

There are numerous techniques for improving service processes, but here we will explain Quality Function Deployment (QFD).

① Philosophy of Quality Function Deployment

It seeks to design products that ensure customer satisfaction and value from beginning to end

② Basic Concept of Quality Function Deployment

It involves translating customer requirements into technical characteristics of a product, and then further translating these into component characteristics, process characteristics, and specific specifications and activities in production. For QFD to be effective, market research results must be accurate, and ambiguous customer needs must be concretely and feasibly documented.

③ Purpose and Advantages of Quality Function Deployment

The goal is to shorten the development period of new products while simultaneously improving product quality. To achieve this, marketing, technical, and production departments must closely collaborate from the early stages of new product development.

QFD helps service providers deliver the service quality that customers demand. By involving customers in the early stages of service development, the design can be tailored to meet customer needs. In other words, it is a methodology in quality management that maximizes customer satisfaction by reflecting customer requirements in the company's products.

The advantages of QFD are as follows:

a. It enables the design to meet customer requirements, thereby understanding customer needs.

b. It can lead to reduced design changes, shortened product development periods, and fewer post-sales defects.

c. It improves teamwork through close cooperation between departments.

d. It allows documentation of all processes using the House of Quality (HOQ).

e. If new characteristics or problems arise during the development stage, they can be applied in the HOQ, allowing early consideration of various alternatives and repeated application of modifications.

④ Steps of Quality Function Implementation

Planning–Design Stage	Calculate the requirements and their importance through methods such as surveys, and enter them into the deployment chart to determine the importance of planning quality and required quality.
Component Deployment	The purpose of component deployment is to expand the subsystems or components related to the critical quality characteristics identified in the previous stage. By evaluating the impact of each component on the system through a matrix between the quality characteristic deployment chart and the component deployment chart, this stage clarifies which components should be managed with priority to achieve the critical quality characteristic goals.
Process Deployment	The major components identified in the previous stage are used to derive the processes that need to be managed with priority among the key processes. The purpose is to identify the processes related to quality characteristics.

⑤ House of Quality

   a. Significance: The House of Quality is a key tool in QFD analysis, arranged in a matrix format to effectively communicate customer requirements identified through market research to production engineers in the technical world.

   b. Components: The components of the House of Quality include customer requirements, interactions, quality characteristics, correlations, design quality, and competitive comparisons.

(7) Five Efforts for Redesigning Service Processes

① Eliminate Steps that Do Not Contribute to Value Creation

② Transition to Self-Service

③ Direct Delivery of Services to Customers

④ Bundled Services

⑤ Redesign the Physical Aspects of the Service Process

Formation of Loyalty → Positive Word of Mouth

   a. Consumption Stage (Service Encounter Stage)

     • Continuous communication with customers

     • Adjust services to meet customer expectations: Efforts to provide customer-centric services

     • Explain reasons when service modifications are necessary

   b. Post-Purchase Stage (Post-Purchase Customer Expectation Management Strategy)

     • Verify whether customer expectations are met: Check customer reactions through feedback processes

     • Develop follow-up aftercare programs: Encourage repeat purchases and help manage future expectations

9.4 ⊷ Customer Satisfaction and Word of Mouth

(1) Introduction to Word of Mouth (WOM)

① Definition: Word of Mouth (WOM) involves the informal sharing of opinions and experiences about products, services, or experiences among individuals. Word of Mouth (WOM) has transitioned from informal, face-to-face exchanges in early societies to a key element in contemporary marketing and consumer behavior. Early research, such as Lazarsfeld and Katz's (1955)[53] study on opinion leaders, demonstrated that certain individuals have a substantial influence on others through their personal recommendations and opinions. Their work highlighted how personal influence operates within communication processes, setting a foundational understanding of how interpersonal communication and opinion leadership can affect public opinion and behavior.

② Significance: As technology advanced, the scope and impact of WOM evolved dramatically. The advent of digital communication and social media has expanded WOM beyond face-to-face interactions. Nowadays, Electronic Word of Mouth (eWOM) refers to the online dissemination of opinions and reviews through platforms such as social media, review sites, and forums. eWOM encompasses various forms of online feedback, including user-generated content and digital reviews, which can reach a global audience instantly. WOM can profoundly affect a business's reputation, customer trust, and overall success. Positive WOM can boost

---

53) Katz, E., & Lazarsfeld, P. F. (1955). *Personal Influence: The Part Played by People in the Flow of Mass Communications*. Free Press.

credibility and attract new patrons, whereas negative WOM can harm a brand's image and dissuade potential customers.

(2) Role of WOM in Tourism and Hospitality

① Influence on Decision—Making: Travelers often depend on recommendations from friends, family, and online reviews when selecting destinations, lodgings, and services. WOM can significantly influence booking decisions and foster brand loyalty.

② Social Proof: Positive testimonials and reviews act as social proof, validating the quality of services and experiences. This is particularly impactful in tourism and hospitality, where personal experiences are highly valued.

③ Building Loyalty: Positive WOM helps build customer loyalty by creating emotional bonds and reinforcing trust in the brand. Loyal customers are more inclined to recommend the business and return for future services.

④ Enhancing Brand Equity: A robust reputation supported by positive WOM can enhance brand equity, distinguishing the business from competitors and adding value to the brand.

(3) Case Studies on eWOM in Tourism Industry

Study	Authors	Overview	Findings
Understanding Customer Experience and Satisfaction through Airline Passengers' Online Reviews[54]	Hyun-Jeong Ban & Hak-Seon Kim	Examines how online reviews reflect customer experiences in the airline industry.	Key aspects include service quality, in-flight amenities, and customer service. Negative reviews often mention delays and poor complaint handling.
Cruising in Asia: What Can We Learn from Online Cruiser Reviews to Understand Their Experience and Satisfaction[55]	Shuting Tao & Hak-Seon Kim	Looks into cruising experiences in Asia via online traveler reviews.	Satisfaction factors include onboard amenities, entertainment, and value for money. Complaints often concern dining options and excursions.
Understanding Customer Experience and Satisfaction of Casino Hotels in Busan through Online User-Generated Content[56]	Wei Fu, Shengnan Wei, Jue Wang, & Hak-Seon Kim	Analyzes user-generated content related to casino hotels in Busan to assess guest satisfaction.	Valued aspects include gaming experiences, luxury accommodations, and customer service. Common complaints are noise levels and equipment condition.
Analyzing Online Reviews to Uncover Customer Satisfaction Factors in Indian Cultural Tourism Destinations[57]	Aura Lydia Riswanto, Seieun Kim, & Hak-Seon Kim	Focuses on cultural tourism in India, analyzing online reviews to identify key satisfaction factors.	Important factors are cultural authenticity, guide quality, and overall visitor experience. Complaints include overcrowding and inadequate guide information.

54) Ban, H., & Kim, H. (2019). Understanding Customer Experience and Satisfaction through Airline Passengers' Online Review. *Sustainability (Switzerland), 11*(15), 1-17.

55) Tao, S., & Kim, H. S. (2019). Cruising in Asia: What can we dig from online cruiser reviews to understand their experience and satisfaction. *Asia Pacific Journal of Tourism Research, 24*(6), 514-528.

56) Fu, W., Wei, S., Wang, J., & Kim, H. S. (2022). Understanding the Customer Experience and Satisfaction of Casino Hotels in Busan through Online User-Generated Content. *Sustainability (Switzerland), 14*(10), 1-18.

57) Riswanto, A. L., Kim, S., & Kim, H. S. (2023). Analyzing Online Reviews to Uncover Customer Satisfaction Factors in Indian Cultural Tourism Destinations. *Behavioral Sciences, 13*(11), 1-15.

(4) Strategies for Leveraging WOM in Tourism and Hospitality

① Encouraging Positive Reviews: Deliver exceptional service and solicit feedback from satisfied customers. Consider offering review incentives or loyalty programs to encourage positive sharing.

② Monitoring and Managing Online Reputation: Utilize reputation management tools to monitor online reviews and social media mentions. Respond promptly to both positive and negative feedback to show engagement and resolve issues.

③ Utilizing User-Generated Content: Feature user-generated content such as photos and testimonials on your website and social media. This enhances credibility and can attract new customers.

(5) WOM Future Direction

① Real-Time Feedback Systems: Future studies could explore the impact of real-time feedback systems on customer satisfaction and service recovery. Investigating the effects of immediate responses on overall satisfaction and loyalty could provide valuable insights. Key areas include:

- The effectiveness of real-time feedback in boosting customer satisfaction.
- How timely responses to feedback affect customer loyalty and retention.
- Strategies for incorporating real-time feedback mechanisms into existing service systems.

② Cultural Differences and Satisfaction: Research could investigate how cultural differences influence customer satisfaction and review trends. Understanding these variations can help businesses tailor their services to diverse markets. Potential areas of focus include:

- Differences in customer satisfaction across various cultural contexts.
- How cultural norms and values impact service expectations and review behaviors.
- Best practices for adapting services to meet the needs of a culturally diverse clientele.

③ Impact of Artificial Intelligence (AI) on Customer Service: Future research could examine the role of AI in enhancing customer service and satisfaction. AI tools such as chatbots, virtual assistants, and predictive analytics are becoming increasingly prevalent. Key research areas include:

- The effectiveness of AI-driven customer service tools in resolving issues and improving satisfaction.
- Customer perceptions of AI interactions compared to human interactions.
- The impact of AI on personalized service delivery and its relationship with customer loyalty.
- Ethical considerations and transparency in AI-driven customer service.

④ Emotional Intelligence in Service Interactions: Research could explore the influence of emotional intelligence (EI) in customer service interactions on overall satisfaction. EI among service employees can greatly affect customer experiences. Key areas of interest include:

- The role of EI in managing challenging customer interactions and enhancing satisfaction.
- The effectiveness of training programs designed to develop EI among service staff.
- The impact of EI on building positive customer relationships and fostering brand loyalty.

About the Author ━━━━━━━━━━━━━━━━━━━━━━━━━━━●

Hak-Seon Kim

Education	Ph.D., Texas Tech University
	M.S., Seoul National University
	B.S., Seoul National University
Career	Dean of Global College
	Professor, School of Hospitality & Tourism Management
	Director, Wellness and Tourism Big Data Research Institute
	Kyungsung University

Seieun (Celine) Kim

Education	Doctoral Student, Kyungsung University
	M.S., Kyungsung University
	B.Eng., Dong-A University
Career	Lecturer, School of Global Studies
	Kyungsung University

Aura Lydia Riswanto

Education	Doctoral Student, Kyungsung University
	M.S., Kyungsung University
	B.A., Kyungsung University
Career	Lecturer, School of Global Studies
	Kyungsung University

Angellie Williady

Education	Doctoral Student, Kyungsung University
	M.S., Kyungsung University
	BS.c., University of Sunderland
Career	Lecturer, School of Global Studies
	Kyungsung University

Hyun-Jeong (Helena) Ban

Education	Ph.D., Kyungsung University
	M.S., Pukyong National University
	B.A., Youngsan University
Career	Assistant Professor, School of Global Studies
	Kyungsung University

Global Service Management: Principles and Practices

2024. 9. 6. 1st edition publish

Author   Hak-Seon Kim, Seieun Kim, Aura L. Riswanto, Angellie Williady, & Hyun-Jeong Ban
Publisher Uk-Sang Chin.
Editor   Haeng-Bok Oh.
Designer Jeong-Eun Oh.
BAEKSAN Publishing Co., Ltd.

370 Hoedong-ro, Paju City, Gyeonggi Province, Republic of Korea
TEL   +82.2.914.1621.
FAX   +82.31.955.9911.
E-mail   edit@ibaeksan.kr
Homepage www.ibaeksan.kr

ISBN   979-11-6567-913-2 93320
Price   **19,000won**